D0222784

RENEWALS 458-4574.

DATE DUE

Frontispiece Anna Halprin at Stinson Beach, California, 2003. Photograph by Rick Chapman, San Francisco

ANNA HALPRIN

Routledge Performance Practitioners is a series of introductory guides to the key theatre-makers of the last century. Each volume explains the background to and the work of one of the major influences on twentieth- and twenty-first-century performance.

Anna Halprin's radical approach to dance as an accessible and life-enhancing art has significantly influenced the development of twentieth-century performance practice.

This volume is the first to combine:

- an overview of Halprin's life and the evolution of her work over the past 60 years
- investigation of her methodology including the Life/Art Process, RSVP Cycles for collective creativity and the Five Stages of Healing
- analysis of her community performance rituals *Circle the Earth* and *The Planetary Dance*
- an experiential approach to Halprin's work through movement explorations and scores.

As a first step towards critical understanding, and as an initial exploration before going on to further, primary research, **Routledge Performance Practitioners** are unbeatable value for today's student.

Helen Poynor is an international movement artist specializing in environmental, site-specific and cross-disciplinary performance, and senior lecturer in theatre and performance at the University of Plymouth. **Libby Worth** is a movement practitioner focusing on collaborative art processes and site-specific theatre, and a lecturer in theatre practice at Royal Holloway, University of London. Both authors trained with Anna Halprin in the early 1980s.

ROUTLEDGE PERFORMANCE PRACTITIONERS

Series editor: Franc Chamberlain, University of Northampton

Routledge Performance Practitioners is an innovative series of introductory handbooks on key figures in twentieth-century performance practice. Each volume focuses on a theatre-maker whose practical and theoretical work has in some way transformed the way we understand theatre and performance. The books are carefully structured to enable the reader to gain a good grasp of the fundamental elements underpinning each practitioner's work. They will provide an inspiring springboard for future study, unpacking and explaining what can initially seem daunting.

The main sections of each book cover:

- personal biography
- explanation of key writings
- description of significant productions
- reproduction of practical exercises.

Volumes currently available in the series are:

Eugenio Barba by Jane Turner
Augusto Boal by Frances Babbage
Michael Chekhov by Franc Chamberlain
Anna Halprin by Libby Worth and Helen Poynor
Jacques Lecoq by Simon Murray
Vsevolod Meyerhold by Jonathan Pitches
Konstantin Stanislavsky by Bella Merlin

Future volumes will include:

Pina Bausch
Bertolt Brecht
Peter Brook
Etienne Decroux
Jerzy Grotowski
Joan Littlewood
Ariane Mnouchkine
Lee Strasberg
Robert Wilson

ANNA HALPRIN

Libby Worth *and* Helen Poynor

Routledge
Taylor & Francis Group

LONDON AND NEW YORK

First published 2004
by Routledge
2 Park Square, Milton Park, Abingdon, Oxon OX14 4RN

Simultaneously published in the USA and Canada
by Routledge
270 Madison Ave, New York, NY 10016

Routledge is an imprint of the Taylor & Francis Group

© 2004 Libby Worth and Helen Poynor

Typeset in Perpetua by
Florence Production Ltd, Stoodleigh, Devon
Printed and bound in Great Britain by
TJ International Ltd, Padstow, Cornwall

British Library Cataloguing in Publication Data
A catalogue record for this book is available from the British
Library

Library of Congress Cataloging in Publication Data
Worth, Libby, 1955–
    Anna Halprin/Libby Worth and Helen Poynor.
        p. cm. – (Routledge performance practitioners)
    Includes bibliographical references and index.
    1. Halprin, Anna.   2. Dancers – United States – Biography.
    3. Modern dance.   4. Dance therapy.   I. Poynor, Helen.
    II. Title.   III. Series.
    GV1785.H267W67 2004
    792.8′092–dc22   2004006007

ISBN 0–415–27329–3 (hbk)
ISBN 0–415–27330–7 (pbk)

CONTENTS

FIGURES

ACKNOWLEDGEMENTS

We are indebted to Anna Halprin and deeply grateful for her generosity of spirit in sharing her resources, including access to her personal archive, supplying illustrations and video recordings and the opportunity to participate in *The Planetary Dance*, and for making time available in her busy schedule for extensive interviews and answering our emails.

We would like to express our thanks to our partners, families, friends and colleagues for their support and understanding about our preoccupation and lack of availability while we were working on this book.

We would also like to thank the following individuals for their generous help in supplying illustrations or written material, or for interviews or supporting us in a myriad of other ways: Duane Beeson, Caroline Born, Ernest Braun, Paul Brill, Rick Chapman, Susanka Christmann, Jay Graham, Charlene Koonce Broudy, Marsha McMann Paludan, Ken Otter, Annie Pfingst, Paul Ryan, Eeo Stubblefield and Jenny Wright.

Special thanks go to Taira Restar for her drawing, help with gathering photographs and for being our link person in California.

We would also like to thank our editors Franc Chamberlain and Talia Rogers for their support.

We gratefully acknowledge permission given by the following to publish extracts and illustrations from books: Wesleyan University Press for the use of material for Figures 1.3, 2.3, 4.1 and 4.2.

LifeRhythm for the use of extracts on pp. 155 and 170. From *Dance as a Healing Art*, by Anna Halprin. Used with permission from the publisher, LifeRhythm, PO Box 806, Mendocino CA 95460, USA, www.LifeRhythm.com.

Every effort has been made to trace the copyright owners of the photographs used from Anna Halprin's archive with her permission. We apologize for any inadvertent errors or omissions and will correct these in future editions if brought to our attention.

AUTHORS' NOTE

Since we both trained with Anna Halprin and her team at the San Francisco Dancers' Workshop/Tamalpa Institute in the early 1980s and have applied the experience and skills gained there in our professional practice over the past 20 years, we are inevitably advocates of her approach. We hope that this perspective helps to clarify some common misapprehensions and contributes to the body of knowledge available about her work.

Some of the archival material available is inconsistent and, while we have done all we can to confirm factual information, we apologize for any errors, which are our own.

LIFE AND WORK

FAMILY BACKGROUND

In 1994, at the age of 73, Anna Halprin made an unexpected return to the public stage. Invited to perform at a Festival of Jewish Artists at the Cowell Theater in San Francisco, Halprin created a solo performance inspired by her Jewish heritage. This piece, which became known as *The Grandfather Dance,* was subsequently performed at the American Dance Festival in 1997 and at Halprin's *80th Year Retrospective* in 2000. Although Halprin had never stopped dancing and creating dances, for more than 20 years her attention had been turned away from theatrical performance and focused on the inter-relationships between artistic and personal process, dance and healing and the creation of contemporary community dance rituals. It is significant that *The Grandfather Dance,* which heralds the almost coincidental blossoming of a late and remarkable phase of Halprin's artistic career, is autobiographical. The dance celebrates her relationship with her grandfather; it is dedicated to her grandchildren to help them appreciate their cultural roots. Halprin's grandfather and his family had been forced to flee the Russian pogroms and, along with many other Jewish immigrants, had settled in Chicago establishing a tailoring business. Lacking a common language, the loving relationship Halprin had with her grandfather who spoke Yiddish was expressed primarily through body language and touch. *The Grandfather*

Dance, performed in her father's elegant pyjamas with a white silk shawl reminiscent of her grandfather's prayer shawl, tells of her weekly childhood visits to her grandfather's synagogue. The young Halprin, whose own life was relatively assimilated in mainstream American culture, was captivated by her grandfather's passionate and embodied prayer and his personal sense of relationship with God. Interpreting his prayer as a dance she concluded that 'God was a dancer' and subsequently claimed that she has spent her life attempting to create dances which were as meaningful as her grandfather's (Halprin with Kaplan 1995: 2). Certainly a potent combination of expressive physicality, emotion and spirituality has characterized much of Halprin's work.

Ann Schuman was born in 1920 and grew up in Winnetka, Illinois. Although named after her maternal grandmother Hannah, a fact that she only discovered many years later, Halprin was known at home (and professionally until 1972) as Ann. Ann was the youngest child and only daughter of a close and supportive family. An unconventional child, Ann danced from the age of three, her natural expressiveness finding an outlet in classes based on the approach of Isadora Duncan (1878–1927) after a less than promising start with a teacher of Russian Ballet (McMann Paludan 1995: 24). Halprin's love of dance was nurtured by her mother who encouraged her to experience many different approaches to dance. Her physicality was also evident in sport at which she excelled and tree-climbing exploits with her two older brothers. Halprin's upbringing appears to have given her the security and self-confidence to develop a clear sense of herself from an early age. Her Jewish background made her aware of her 'difference' and a concomitant need to prove herself in the mainstream American culture which was her social milieu. At the same time Halprin claims this sense of difference proved liberating later in her career when her pioneering work flew in the face of the establishment. Halprin's family was involved in social issues and she attributes her social conscience to a Jewish sense of responsibility. Several of her early dances reflect her concern with world issues on the brink of the Second World War. In 1939 she created a dance on the theme of war and refugees, and in 1940 another on liberty and freedom. An earlier dance in 1938 inspired by the beauty of nature highlighted the significance of her early relationship to the natural environment (Halprin *c.*1938–40).

EARLY YEARS

Halprin's childhood passion for dance developed throughout her teens as she continued classes and created her own dances to be performed at school and in Chicago, including her first solo *Saga of Youth*. With her mother's continued support Halprin's dance education touched on a range of modern dance techniques based on the styles of eminent choreographers of the period, such as Isadora Duncan and Ruth St Denis (1879–1968). In 1936, while studying at the University of California, she choreographed *Pastorale* in which she danced using music 'with contrasting themes of improvised circular and angular movement' (McMann Paludan 1995: 25). These early performances which drew on an eclectic mix of dance influences allowed Halprin to experiment with her own style and content. So that, at the summer workshop in 1937 at Bennington College, she already had a basis from which to evaluate the experience of working with major modern dance techniques prominent in America at that time.

In 1934, 'Bennington College, a new women's school in Vermont, created the nation's first center for modern dance. The summer program consisted of a school and a series of concerts given by the faculty' (Mazo 2000: 136), which rapidly gained a reputation for providing expert teaching in a range of modern dance forms attracting the best known dancers to its staff. These included Martha Graham (1894–1991), Doris Humphrey (1895–1958), Charles Weidman (1901–75), Hanya Holm (1893–1992) (who had worked closely with German modern expressionist dancer Mary Wigman (1886–1973)) and Louis Horst (1884–1964) (musician, composer and dance composition teacher). While open to discovery of other dancers' techniques and styles, even at such a young age Halprin did not feel driven by what she had experienced to settle into one form of training. At Bennington, Doris Humphrey spotted Halprin's dance talent and asked her to join the Humphrey–Weidman Company in New York City. However, difficult as it was to reject such a prestigious offer, Halprin recollects of the period 'I had promised my family I would graduate from college before I became a professional dancer, so I decided to postpone this opportunity until I had finished school' (Ross 2000: xv). Of the two colleges in America that offered a dance major Halprin chose Bennington and was initially disappointed to be turned down and to have to take up a place instead at the University of Wisconsin. However, this turned out to be 'the luckiest mishap of my life. It was at the University of Wisconsin that I met the two people who would most influence my dance career: my future husband, Lawrence Halprin [1916–ㅤ], and my mentor, Margaret H'Doubler [1889–1982]' (Ross 2000: xv).

MARGARET H'DOUBLER AND DANCE AT WISCONSIN

Halprin enrolled at the University of Wisconsin in 1938 and studied there for four and a half years, clearly exhilarated and inspired primarily by Margaret H'Doubler's teaching. Although not a dancer herself, H'Doubler had become an enthusiastic advocate for the value of dance in education. Many of the principles she adhered to became foundational in Halprin's development, an indebtedness that Halprin, in her eighties, continues to acknowledge.

Recognized as a pioneer in the field of dance education, having set up the first undergraduate dance degree in the world in 1926 at Wisconsin, H'Doubler was initially a scientist with a degree in biology. She taught physical education at the University of Wisconsin and had an enthusiasm for basketball. The particular combination of values and skills she brought together in the creation of the dance degree was to influence directly and indirectly generations of dance teachers and to a lesser extent dance performers and choreographers. The formulation of the degree had its origins in a period of research at Columbia University and in New York City in 1916. Here H'Doubler came into contact with two teachers who used a scientific approach to dance and elements of improvisation, while a music teacher she met had students lie on the floor and begin to move from that position (Ross 2000: 118–19). 'H'Doubler suddenly realized that lying on the floor, removed from the pull of gravity, it was at last possible to get the body to move with true freedom . . .' (Ross 2000: 119–20).

In addition she became absorbed in the work of John Dewey (1859–1952), an educationalist and philosopher in the Department of Philosophy and Psychology at Columbia. His advocacy of the importance of experience in the learning process had obvious applications to the teaching of dance. This was combined with a theory of knowledge based on problem solving long used in the sciences, but according to Dewey, just as relevant in the teaching of the arts. In his view any inquiry or reflection would 'have the same pattern of steps'. 'It would begin with a problem and proceed through testing of possible solutions, to a resolution' (Ross 2000: 125).

Although Halprin studied with H'Doubler well after her initial establishment of the dance degree, the type of class she experienced was still based on the philosophical principles H'Doubler had encountered in her studies with John Dewey. H'Doubler was determined to take a holistic approach to the teaching of dance, like Dewey avoiding a mind/body split and recognizing the significance of the physical, emotional, spiritual and intellectual components of dance. In her book *Dance – A Creative Art Experience* completed while Halprin was at Wisconsin, H'Doubler makes a strong case for the role of dance in education, stressing its value for developing the personality: 'It serves all the ends of individual growth; it helps to develop the body; it stimulates the imagination and challenges the intellect; it helps cultivate an appreciation for beauty; it deepens and refines the emotional nature' (H'Doubler 1940: 64).

As Halprin would do later, she argued for the need for accessible dance and abhorred the thrust she had observed in New York for forms that were becoming tightly codified and refined, resulting in an reductive process that generated increasingly less involvement in dance. She wanted 'to revive, through some kind of movement education, the impulse to move expressively, to dance, to develop adequate techniques for artistic expression' (H'Doubler 1940: 44).

Ross notes in her book on H'Doubler that '[t]he shift to valuing the process over the product was one of Dewey's ideas that underlay H'Doubler's whole philosophy of dance education' (Ross 2000: 129). Dance students at Wisconsin undertook a pre-medical course to increase their knowledge of anatomy and scientific principles. H'Doubler built on this and encouraged her students to learn experientially about the structural make-up of the body and its capacity for movement. Their control developed through increased kinaesthetic awareness aiding creative expression. Alongside explorations into the spatial, rhythmic and dynamic elements of dance, H'Doubler insisted on the value of the emotional and imaginative experience of movement. She encouraged her students to have a sense of connection with the natural world through dancing outside. In order for dancers to follow the innate 'craving for expression and the sharing of the enhanced emotional state' (H'Doubler 1940: 53) they must both 'train the mind to use the body and to reflect its conditions . . . and train the body to be responsive to the expressive mind' (H'Doubler 1940: 70). As Halprin recalls, this style of teaching allowed students to explore 'all the possibilities a movement could yield. This self-discovery evoked qualities, feelings, and images. Out of these personal responses we would then create our own dance experience' (Ross 2000: xvi).

Both H'Doubler and Halprin drew on the pioneering work of Mabel E. Todd (1856–1932) who, in 1937, published her seminal work *The Thinking Body*, a book that continues to inform and inspire dancers and teachers of dance. It is based on the principle that: 'The individual is a totality and cannot be segregated as to intellect, motor and social factors. They are all interrelated' (Todd 1968: 3). Todd proceeded to analyse the relationship between these factors in great detail. Drawing on the work from a variety of fields such as science, engineering, medicine, anthropology and psychology, she explored the impact that thinking and feeling have on the basic structure of the body and way that we move. Of particular value in her work for Halprin was the emphasis on visualization, imagination and tasks to explore her 'psychophysical' theories. For instance she examined the specific difficulties a person has to overcome in walking, by virtue of the fact that they stand upright on two legs in a field of gravity. She considered anatomical facts in relation to mechanical forces while simultaneously extolling the importance of visual images and psychological attitude in encouraging ease and efficiency in movement.

While at Wisconsin, Halprin recalls in interview that her 'reconnection with Judaism and Rabbi Kadushin was a reaction to the Hitler era' (McMann Paludan 1995: 35). She became politically active in the Jewish student organization, the Hillel Foundation led by Rabbi Kadushin, and found support here and through H'Doubler for performance work and her senior dance project on the history of Jewish dance.

LAWRENCE HALPRIN AND THE BAUHAUS CONNECTION

In 1939 Ann Schuman met Lawrence Halprin, a graduate from Cornell University who had come to Wisconsin to study botany but realized while there that he wanted to focus on landscape architecture. They married in 1940 and while Anna Halprin completed her dance studies, Lawrence having finished his Ph.D. went to study at the Harvard School of Architecture in Cambridge. On joining her husband, Anna Halprin's interest was sparked by the work of Walter Gropius (1883–1968) who was then teaching at Harvard. Gropius had led the

German Bauhaus movement of the 1920s and established a teaching institution for the arts at Weimer (director 1919–28) consisting of a collection of workshops and a self-contained community of teachers and students who 'embraced the whole range of visual arts: architecture, planning, painting, sculpture, industrial design and stage work' (Gropius 1961: 1). Given Anna Halprin's recent experience of study with H'Doubler and Mabel Todd it is hardly surprising that she felt drawn to sit in on lectures given by Gropius who stated:

> One of the fundamental maxims of the Bauhaus was the demand that the teacher's own approach was never to be imposed on the student; that, on the contrary, any attempt at imitation by the student was to be ruthlessly suppressed. The stimulation received from the teacher was only to help him find his bearings.
>
> (Gropius 1961: 1)

Alongside the dance teaching Halprin had organized at the Windsor prep school and volunteer work in two settlement homes, she sat in on design courses, 'transposed the design problems into choreographic studies and found interested architecture students to study dance with her' (McMann Paludan 1995: 37). The Bauhaus principles of cross-art collaboration, collective creativity and the integration of art in society and in everyday life were to remain fundamental aspects in the development of both Anna's and Lawrence's artistic careers.

The Bauhaus ideal that encouraged workshop experimentation and democratic group work rather than artist as hero, reinforced Halprin's experiences with H'Doubler at Wisconsin. However, during this period, while Lawrence Halprin left to serve in the navy during the Second World War, Anna Halprin still identified herself as a modern dancer. By chance, an opportunity arose for her to audition for Doris Humphrey and Charles Weidman, who had reunited to choreograph a musical *Sing Out, Sweet Land*. Halprin could now take up the offer she had turned down before Wisconsin and become a part of a dance company run by Humphrey and Weidman. She was promoted to female lead and performed in Boston (1944) and subsequently in New York. For several years she worked on this and other similar musical productions gaining a reputation as a successful dance comedienne.

During the 1940s Halprin continued to experiment with her own style of dance including choreographing *The Prophetess* and *Lonely Ones*

(1946). She performed these at the YMCA Annual Young Choreographers' Concert, where John Cage (1912–92), the avant-garde
American composer, was impressed with her work and introduced her
to dancer/choreographer Merce Cunningham (1919–). The friendship
that was established in New York was maintained once the Halprins
moved to San Francisco, with Cage and Cunningham visiting to teach
classes and give informal performances on the dance deck at her studio
in Kentfield (McMann Paludan 1995: 42).

Figure 1.1 *The Prophetess*, 1955. Photograph by Ernest Braun

THE MOVE TO SAN FRANCISCO

As Lawrence Halprin acknowledges, his wish to settle in San Francisco after the War in 1945 was not so welcome to Anna. 'She felt that the centre for dance was in New York City and from her point of view at that time I think she made a great sacrifice' (*Lawrence and Anna Halprin, Inner Landscapes* 1991). Anna Halprin's initial experience of living in San Francisco was to confirm her view that there was little dance to interest her in the immediate vicinity. However, a chance meeting with a Martha Graham trained dancer, Welland Lathrop, led to the establishment of a joint studio in the city for teaching adults and children, alongside the development of their own choreography for concert performances. The two dancers' styles of working were very different which had the advantage of attracting a wide range of people to the studio. Halprin took main responsibility for the children's work and in doing so began a particularly fertile period of research through teaching, that resulted in her being 'instrumental in developing the Marin Dance Co-operatives (1947)' (Halprin 1995: 25). In 1948 Halprin founded *Impulse*, a magazine that became a forum for writing on emerging dance practices. In the same year she travelled to the newly formed country of Israel for the first time where she was introduced to the movement practitioner Moshe Feldenkrais (1904–84), whose work immediately appealed to her and whose friendship she valued.

THE MARIN DANCE CO-OPERATIVES

Through the Marin Dance Co-operatives (1947), Halprin 'taught dance for the next twenty-five years to children in the community' where she lived (Halprin 1995: 25). From the start of the Co-op, Halprin recognized the importance of 'the holistic nature of working with the child' and of integrating family and school experience in the classes. Parents were brought in as assistants and the school curriculum or major events were translated into dances or rituals that were shared with other groups and parents at performance festivals. This first experience of working with a community was well received in Marin and had the added benefit of extending her own development as a dancer, teacher and choreographer. From as early as 1948 a clear set of principles guided the teaching, including that classes were to be cheap and open to all since 'every child and adult who can move, can dance' (Halprin 1948). Classes were run somewhat on the H'Doublerian model of stimulation to encourage learning through personal kinaesthetic investigation rather than mimicry of a single dance style. Instructions were formulated to 'simultaneously cultivate physical skill, together with the emotional and intellectual spheres of activity' (Halprin 1948). Basic movements were explored such as running, jumping and skipping in a non-judgemental atmosphere where learning to value each other's differences took precedence over grading performance. Halprin's recollection of one boy demonstrates the value she placed on self-motivation and experiential learning. He 'galloped for about six weeks in a row, that's all he did because every time he galloped he got some new little insight about galloping' (Halprin 2001b). Halprin struggled to find the right structural balance for the classes to support spontaneity while maintaining stimulation and motivation (Halprin 2001b). This provided useful experience for later work on closed and open instructions for improvisation with co-dancers and artists. Halprin's interest in the dramatic content of the classes distinguished her work from H'Doubler's, as did her preference for working with time in relation to space rather than as she had done at Wisconsin 'in terms of the meter system' (McMann Paludan 1995: 53).

THE MOVE AWAY FROM MODERN DANCE

The Halprins moved out of San Francisco to Kentfield, into a house designed by Bill Woorster in collaboration with Lawrence Halprin on a five acre wooded site on the slopes of Mount Tamalpais. With the birth of their daughters Daria (1948) and Rana (1951), Halprin spent less time at the Halprin–Lathrop studio in order to concentrate on family life and on increasingly important research she was conducting into dance at her home studio. The final split with both the Halprin–Lathrop studio and with modern dance came at the end of 1955. She had previously danced two of her solos *The Prophetess* and *Madrone* on the outdoor dance deck built beneath her home as audition pieces for Martha Graham, who was touring America in order to assemble performances for the Festival of American Dance in New York. Halprin's dances were selected and she travelled to New York to join a prestigious gathering of modern dance performers from around America, seemingly a valuable forum for Halprin after her relatively secluded period on the West Coast. Martha Graham 'supplied Halprin with a rehearsal space and costuming advice' and her performances were well received (McMann Paludan 1995: 59) yet her actual experience was the reverse of stimulating. For the two weeks of performances she noticed that 'all the dancers looked like imitations of the leading choreographer. I wasn't able to connect. I felt depressed, discouraged, distrustful, and I knew that my career as a modern dancer had just died' (Halprin 1981: 14).

On return from New York, she left the studio she had run with Welland Lathrop and threw herself into detailed research on the basics of dance. Lawrence Halprin and Arch Lauterer designed a dance deck beneath the Halprins' house in Kentfield making an outdoor studio that became a major source of inspiration for dance research and teaching. Originally designed to overcome the prohibitive expense and difficulty of building a large indoor studio on such steep wooded slopes, Anna Halprin wrote of the deck that it 'floats in a ravine surrounded by red-wood and madrone trees on the slopes of Mount Tamalpais. The deck breaks rectangular shape and reaches into the woods in a meandering fashion' (Halprin 1988: 1), with different levels and low stepped benches on one side for seating it provides a versatile and stimulating space. Halprin appreciated the 'deep and lasting effect' the deck had on her work as it 'removed the usual restrictions and added elements of nature and chance and, with them, a lack of control and predictability' (Halprin 1988: 1). Here Halprin was able to follow her own movement explorations, gradually drawing other dancers and artists of different disciplines interested in improvisation to work with her. 'The space is full of trees, rocks, uneven surfaces and textures. Here we have to accommodate our movements to the space itself. This was the origin of task movements' (Halprin 1988: 1).

THE SAN FRANCISCO DANCERS' WORKSHOP

EARLY WORK 1955–65

The Dancers' Workshop was initiated by Anna Halprin with a group of dancers and artists of other disciplines in the early 1950s. In 1955 the group established a base in San Francisco and became known as the San Francisco Dancers' Workshop. The impetus to form this new group grew out of a combination of Halprin's increasing disillusionment with modern dance and the practical circumstances of her life.

The foundations of Halprin's future work began as a series of explorations on her dance deck at her home at the foot of Mount Tamalpais. She established a workshop situation with a group of young artists and dancers from San Francisco, which allowed her the freedom to explore, rather than teach, and to enter unknown territory. She began to actively discard modern dance as a limiting orthodoxy, using improvisation to 'eliminate stereotyped ways of reacting' and release the restrictions imposed by modern dance training and philosophy (Halprin 1995: 77). She returned to anatomy as a basis for the creation of movement. Not only was the form of her work fundamentally different from the modern dance of the era but her basic orientation was at odds with the contemporary assumptions about what constituted dance: 'We began to deal with ourselves as people, not dancers. We incorporated actions that had never been used in dance before' (Halprin 1995: 79). She invited 'visual artists, musicians, actors, architects, poets, psychologists and film-makers' (Halprin 1995: xi) to become collaborators in her explorations. Voice, dialogue, objects and music became an integral part of the work. The quest was 'to rediscover the basic nature of our materials free of preconceived associations and concepts' to avoid 'the predictability of cause and effect' (Halprin 1995: xi). Although the group created performances, the workshop ethos was central to the work, the process of creative questioning and research was as important as the performances generated. Throughout the 25 or more years of its existence the San Francisco Dancers' Workshop never became a repertory company. Two years of process might come to fruition in a single performance before the company moved on to a new phase of exploration or an ephemeral event could be created with little preparation. *Birds of America* (1960) was the first major work produced by the company; it was a manifestation of a system of movement compositions based on anatomical combinations and emphasized the 'non-representational aspects of dance' (Kostelanetz 1970: 67). Immediately before the performance Halprin unexpectedly asked the company to dance holding long bamboo poles, radically changing the spatial environment. This development heralded another phase of Halprin's evolution, signalling her life-long interest in the relationship of movement to the environment.

Five-Legged Stool (1962)

Halprin was concerned that the emphasis on personal kinaesthetic awareness used to develop *Birds of America* had resulted in the work becoming too introspective (Halprin 1995: 81). This is a criticism that could be levelled at some of the subsequent practitioners of postmodern dance for similar reasons. *Five-Legged Stool*, the company's next work, had a radically different focus. The movement vocabulary was generated by physical tasks such as moving 40 wine bottles up into the ceiling or crawling up a diagonal plank and sliding down it head first (Halprin 1995: 83–4). Collaboration with artists from other disciplines became integrated in the process of creating the work. The performers broke away from the restrictions of the proscenium arch and began to use all the space in the theatre building, 'the outside, the corridors, the ceilings, the basement, the aisle, everything . . .' (Halprin 1995: 85). They no longer looked like modern dancers but wore randomly selected costumes and shoes. Halprin had begun to create a new form of 'total theater' (Halprin 1995: 256).

Pre-figuring the work of Pina Bausch (1940–), commonly recognized as the instigator of European Dance Theatre, *Five-Legged Stool* used radical juxtapositions in an attempt to challenge the audiences' habitual associations. Undermining conventional notions of cause and effect, Halprin hoped the audience would respond to her work as a sensory experience rather than intellectually. For her the juxtapositions were without logical meaning but possessed an inherent theatricality and emotional coherence (Kostelanetz 1970: 68–9). Audiences in America and Europe responded to such an audacious challenge to the status quo with outrage and hostility.

Exposizione (1963)

Lucianio Berio, an Italian composer inspired by *Five-Legged Stool* and the creativity of Halprin's work with children, invited the company to collaborate with him creating an 'opera' for the Venice Biennial in 1963. *Exposizione* developed several of the techniques initiated in *Five-Legged Stool*, including the use of the performance environment, task-based movement and juxtapositions. The work was a full-scale collaboration between the dancers, the composer, a sculptor, visual artist Jo Landor and lighting designer Patric Hickey (both of whom had worked on *Five Legged-Stool* and continued to work with Halprin for many years). The scale of the undertaking exceeded anything that Halprin had previously attempted. The performance was created in response to the architecture of the Venice Opera House, which was transformed by a large cargo net suspended 40 foot high across the

Figure 1.2 *Exposizione*, 1963. Photographer unknown, from Anna Halprin's personal archive

proscenium stretching over the orchestra pit and back into the stage, and a ramp creating a slanting floor. The dancers (including Halprin's young daughters, Rana and Daria) were given the task to 'penetrate the entire auditorium' (Halprin 1995: 88) carrying enormous bundles of objects: car tyres, parachutes and a hassock full of tennis balls. The performers' movement was conditioned not only by the environment and their luggage but by the time that had been allocated for each stage of their journey which had to be strictly adhered to. This Herculean task was further complicated by the complex vocal scores written for the dancers in Italian, Greek and English. In addition, the dancers heard the musical score, played by an 18-piece orchestra, for the first time in performance. Each person was 'designed as an object' (Halprin 1995: 91) with the costume intended as an extension of their props, but the costumes were ripped to shreds every performance as a result of the extremity of their tasks. The intensity of the experience for performers and audience alike, with bodies and objects flying through the space, generated an active and vocal response from the audience, and left Halprin with a desire to investigate the nature of 'the encounter' between performers and audience more fully (Halprin 1995: 93).

Parades and Changes (1965–7)

Parades and Changes can be seen as the culmination of this period of work. The complex use of scoring through which it was created had evolved from the earlier works. The performance score was created in collaboration with composer Morton Subotnik who had worked on *Five-Legged Stool*. It consisted of a series of contrasting cellblocks written on cards, created for each of the artistic media: visual, sound, environmental, light and movement. These cellblocks operated independently from each another and were selected and combined in different sequences according to the environment for each performance. The result was 12 different versions of the dance of varying duration created in response to each of the performance venues. The interdisciplinary approach allowed the artists to work collectively across art forms, their roles at times becoming interchangeable. In the 'Paper Dance' the dancers generated a soundscape by tearing huge sheets of paper rolled across the stage, at other times they used their voices, laughing and shouting or stamping their feet percussively. The dancers interacted with elements in the environment including a moveable scaffolding structure and, in one version, a large weather balloon. The New York performance included a goat, which promptly urinated on stage (Hering 1967).

Parades and Changes included an undressing score in which the performers slowly and ritualistically removed and replaced all their clothing while looking first at the audience and then at one another. The movement was not eroticized, the instruction to the performers was to be aware of their responses and their breathing as they carried out the task. For Halprin the dance was not about sexuality (Halprin 2001b) but rather an initiation (Halprin 1981: 16) which reflected an approach to dance, the body and the self. While this section of the dance was perceived as a 'ceremony of trust' when it was performed in Sweden in 1965 (Halprin 1981: 16) it created a furore at the New York performance in 1967 and Halprin narrowly escaped arrest. In some situations the 'Undressing and Dressing Dance' could not be performed; in a performance in Poland (1965) the score was reversed with the dancers

Figure 1.3 *Parades and Changes*, 1965. Photograph by Hank Kranzler, from Anna Halprin's personal archive

progressively adding rather than removing articles of clothing (Halprin 2001b). The outraged response to Halprin's use of nudity had an adverse effect on performance opportunities available to the company in the following years (Halprin 2001b). Nevertheless Halprin has continued to use the naked body in her work when appropriate reflecting her approach to the body and 'natural' movement and the Californian environment in which her work has evolved. The 'Undressing and Dressing Dance' and the 'Paper Dance' were recreated for Halprin's *80th Year Retrospective* in 2000.

Apartment 6 (1965)

In parallel with *Parades and Changes* and in sharp contrast to it, Halprin was developing *Apartment 6* in collaboration with actor John Graham (1930–) and A. A. Leath, a H'Doubler trained dancer, both core members of the Dancers' Workshop with whom she had been working for 14 years. The performance focused on the complex relationships between the three colleagues. Its structure was more unpredictable than *Parades and Changes* (Kostelanetz 1970: 77), for although it highlighted each relationship in turn and the performers carried out specific domestic tasks, such as making pancakes or reading the newspaper, their interactions were improvised in each performance. The authenticity of these interactions was paramount. The performers played themselves using their personal responses as their artistic material, contained and expressed within agreed limitations, for example who could use words or movement in particular situations. Three levels of 'reality' functioned simultaneously: the practical reality of the tasks, the emotional reality of the interactions and the embodiment of fantasies which arose in the moment (Halprin 1995: 98–9). *Apartment 6* was even less identifiable as dance than Halprin's other performances of this period. The intention was radically different to the early kinaesthetic improvisations which had not been concerned with self-expression (Halprin 1995: 77). Like those explorations improvisation is again being used to bypass the limitations of stereotypical or conventional behaviour, but now psychological blocks are being challenged as well as physical and artistic ones.

Apartment 6 was motivated in part by a need to move beyond a potential impasse in the working relationships of the three performers who formed the nucleus of the company (Halprin 1995: 97). While succeeding in its own terms as performance, *Apartment 6* catalysed a parting of the ways which led to significant structural and artistic changes in the Dancers' Workshop. This split was perhaps inevitable given the intensity and personally provocative nature of the working process. After *Apartment 6* Halprin wanted to keep her artistic options open while Graham and Leath wished to continue in the same vein

Figure 1.4 *Apartment 6*, 1965, performance in Helsinki, Finland. Photograph by Ove Alsti, from Anna Halprin's personal archive

(Halprin 2001b). Many years later, in the 1980s, Graham returned to work with Halprin on the training programme at the Tamalpa Institute.

Apartment 6 was the first real attempt to integrate personal and artistic process, which subsequently became a major focus in Halprin's work. The depth of emotional confrontation in the work could not have been achieved without psychological guidance. During this period Halprin became involved with the therapeutic work of Fritz Perls (1893–1970), the founder of Gestalt Therapy (McMann Paludan 1995: 79). Perls worked as a consultant on the piece and became an influential figure in the development of Halprin's future work.

HUMAN POTENTIAL MOVEMENT

Halprin's involvement with the human potential (or growth) movement of the 1960s and 1970s was as influential in the development of her working process as any of the artistic or performance trends of the era. At this time in California there was an explosion of alternative therapies and approaches to the body. Nothing in Halprin's dance training had prepared her for, or equipped her to deal with, the strong emotions which were being provoked in performers and audiences alike once she moved away from the confines of a stylized approach to dance. Inevitably as the Dancers' Workshop began to work holistically and collaboratively rather than within the de-personalized forms and clearly established hierarchies of modern dance, the artists' emotions and the interactions between them began to be exposed. In order to be able to work creatively with this material Halprin needed to gain an understanding of personal and group process and to develop new tools to engage with and transform emotional material and facilitate communication.

Gestalt Therapy was ideally suited to her needs, emphasizing the link between non-verbal behaviour and underlying attitudes and beliefs, and examining the relationship between the use of language and physical expression. Gestalt highlights sensory impressions engendering an in depth body awareness. Its focus on 'here and now' experiences directly contributes to the sense of presence in performance.

The Dancers' Workshop company worked intensively with Perls for several years in the 1960s (Halprin Khalighi 1989: 18). This method of embodying feelings became fundamental to Halprin's creative work. Other techniques such as 'active listening', a tool for communication, and bio-energetic body therapy were also incorporated into her training methods (see Chapter 2). Through Perls, Halprin began to teach at the Esalen Institute, a focal point for the growth of alternative therapies in California where she continues to teach annually. Halprin also created ceremonies for the American humanistic psychology conferences (Halprin 1981).

Halprin came to believe that 'each of us is our own art' and that restrictions in personal/emotional expression would result in corresponding artistic limitations (Halprin 1995: 112). The integration of therapeutic techniques into her creative training reflected Halprin's desire to create 'authentic' performances and laid the foundations for the Life/Art Process which has become the hallmark of Halprin's approach.

ALTERNATIVE APPROACHES TO THE BODY

Throughout her working life Halprin has maintained a lively curiosity about alternative approaches to the body. Concurrently with her use of alternative therapies and inspired by the pre-medical course taken in her early training Halprin investigated many different approaches to body work (Halprin 2001b). She was particularly attracted to the movement and awareness work of Moshe Feldenkrais (see Chapter 2) which has remained a lasting influence, because she felt a kinship between his approach and H'Doubler's.

Halprin's skill at combining and integrating the emotions and alternative approaches to the body in her movement work is central to her contribution to the dance world. While the inclusion of practices such as yoga, the Alexander technique and martial arts in dance training is no longer surprising it was a radical approach in the 1960s and 1970s.

EVOLUTION

By the end of the first ten years of its life the San Francisco Dancers' Workshop had achieved international recognition as an avant-garde performance group. With the break-up of the original core group in the wake of *Apartment 6* and a desire to investigate the relationship between the performers and audiences, significant changes were underway. The company re-emerged as a group of young people that was constantly in a state of flux. The work being created had already begun a process of transformation from recognizable, albeit radical forms of theatrical performance to what Halprin called 'events'. This transformation had been triggered by the extreme audience reactions to the earlier work. Halprin had been taken aback by the energy that had been unleashed and wanted to explore ways of channelling it more constructively. Not content with her research into the personal creative process of her performers, she wanted to explore the interaction between audience and performers. To create work which was 'a collective statement' that involved the audience creatively rather than being 'introspective, private, esoteric and abstract' (Kostelanetz 1970: 74). Early explorations with the original company had included a *Series of Compositions for an Audience* (Halprin 1995: 93).

Myths (1967–8) and other events

In 1967–8 the Dancers' Workshop initiated *Myths*, a series of ten participatory events in the San Francisco studio conceived as 'an experiment in mutual creation' (Halprin 1995: 130). Environments, created in collaboration with Patric Hickey, provided both a stimulus and container for the participants' activities and responses functioning as 'self-directing score(s)' (Halprin 1995: 131). These environments varied according to the theme and intention of the myth. For *Maze*, a 12 foot high labyrinth suspended from a wire grid was constructed from wrapping paper, newspaper and sheets of black, white and clear plastic. For *Creation*, 60 empty chairs were suspended from the walls at different levels above lighted platforms. The environments were combined with simple physical scores which were intended to be 'self-generating' (Halprin 1995: 149). Participants altered the environments through their interaction with them, bodies became environments, recurrent formations of lines and circles were used. The working method of combining movement scores and environments that the Dancers' Workshop had developed as a performing company was now being extended to the participants of *Myths*.

Initially, members of the Dancers' Workshop were the initiators and guides during the events; as the series evolved roles became blurred, the participants becoming performers and the catalysts for one another and the group. Working with archetypal themes each myth generated a different atmosphere and quality of interaction: exuberant, contemplative, intimate, ritualistic and confrontational. In *Atonement*, facing starkly lit walls papered with a repeated page of newspaper, participants made a symbolic gesture to alter their clothing then remained in stillness and silence for an hour contemplating the notion of sin. Halprin saw *Atonement* as an initiation or ordeal; Yom Kippur, the Jewish Day of Atonement, immediately springs to mind. The last myth of the series *Ome* also had strongly spiritual resonances.

The series was in a constant process of evolution, which was unpredictable at times falling into chaos, in *Maze* the group destroyed and rebuilt the whole environment. This response was recycled in the next myth *Dreams* when half the group constructed an environment for the other half to experience. Halprin's task in *Myths* was to create scores which gave individuals the freedom to respond in their own way to the stimulus offered, while providing a strong and flexible enough structure to facilitate the creative engagement of the whole group and to generate a sense of ownership. In her role as director Halprin responded to what was happening in the moment, modifying scores, introducing new ones or integrating suggestions from participants. *Myths* were in every sense 'live' events. The transformation from 'performance' to participatory event demanded an equivalent transformation in the role of the artist, from controlling artistic genius to creative facilitator and collaborator.

The Dancers' Workshop also created events in non-theatre venues. *Bath* (1967), a 'spontaneous theatre piece' created in response to the fountain in a museum courtyard in Connecticut, evolved out of several months of workshop explorations on the theme of bathing. In 1968, in response to an invitation to create a performance for a formal lunch at the Hilton Hotel, the group created a slow motion eating ritual to the bemusement of the other diners.

Halprin was inspired by community events and public ceremonies which she had witnessed when travelling (Kostelanetz 1970: 67). She began to reclaim public places as sites for her work which on several occasions resulted in clashes with the authorities. The Dancers' Workshop staged a march with blank placards through the centre of San Francisco symbolizing their right to perform anywhere in the city, and in *Automobile Event* (1968) used cars in the street as an environment for movement (Halprin 1995: 9, 11). There are parallels between Halprin's work of this era and the 'Happenings' on the East Coast. Halprin aligned her work more closely with the beginnings of performance art and avant-garde theatre than she did with the dance establishment. Like musician John Cage and artist Allan Kaprow (1927–), key figures in the evolution of Happenings, Halprin rejected the restraints of a highly technical training, traditional boundaries between art forms, and the rigid separation between artist and audience or between art and daily life. Her events, like Happenings, disregarded theatrical conventions of time, space and linear narrative, frequently taking place in non-theatre spaces where the environment became a crucial component of the work. Both Happenings and Halprin's events operated as multi-layered experiences where meaning was not prescribed. In both, scores were used to communicate with participants and the activities were frequently task-based, incorporating everyday objects, sounds and movements. Some of the characteristics of Happenings are apparent in Halprin's early performance works, for example the use of illogical juxtaposition and the discrete 'cells' of action in *Parades and Changes* that could be combined or sequenced in different ways. One of the differences between Halprin's events and Happenings is Halprin's growing emphasis on collective creativity and the autonomy of participants and the interaction between them, resulting in a sense of community and group ownership of the event. Increasingly Halprin was concerned with creating events that were meaningful for the individuals participating and served the needs of the community.

While Halprin was undeniably part of the general trend in avant-garde art in the 1960s, and was in communication with artists working on the East Coast, her work had a distinctly West Coast flavour. She responded to the hippy culture which flourished in San Francisco leading a group of 1,000 young people dancing at a Janis Joplin concert in the Haight Ashbury (Halprin with Kaplan 1995: 77). At a another concert by the Grateful Dead, Allen Ginsberg chanted his poetry while members of the Dancers' Workshop painted their bodies in 'intricate fluorescent patterns' and danced among the audience holding aloft plastic sheets on which film images were projected (Halprin 1995: 102). The social and cultural movements of the era were crucial influences on both the form of Halprin's work and the values implicit within it.

THE THEATRICAL AVANT-GARDE

At this time Halprin's work was denigrated by the dance world although she influenced many young dancers who later attracted international attention. But she was recognized as influential by practitioners of avant-garde theatre and performance art resulting in a relationship of mutual interest and exchange. Scores were sent back and forth between Halprin and the Fluxus experimental art group in New York (Halprin 2001b). Julian Beck (1925–85) and Judith Malina (1926–), founders of the Living Theatre, contacted Halprin after seeing *Parades and Changes* on European television. Two of the performers in the New York version subsequently joined the Living Theatre and, in 1968, the two companies worked together at the San Francisco Dancers' Workshop (McMann Paludan 1995: 157). Richard Schechner (1934–) too was quick to recognize the importance of Halprin's work. After the 1967 performance of *Parades and Changes* he invited her to lead a workshop for the nascent Performance Group in New York and attended her workshop at the Esalen Institute in 1968 (McMann Paludan 1995: 151–4). Halprin saw parallels between her work and that of Joseph Chaikin (1935–2003) at the Open Theater, an experimental theatre workshop/company which operated in New York for ten years from the early 1960s. Some members of the Open Theater had studied with Halprin although she only came into direct contact with Chaikin when he moved to the Bay area in 1989 (McMann Paludan 1995: 156). Halprin found the work of Chaikin, Peter Brook (1925–) and Jerzy Grotowski (1933–99) more stimulating than the dance practice of the era. She was attracted to the exploratory nature of Grotowski's work, his changing relationship with the audience and his combination of physical work and text. She eventually met Grotowski when he was working in California in the 1980s and expresses some reservations about his experimentation with emotional material, feeling that there was not a clear enough containing structure or process to conduct such work responsibly (Halprin 2001b). Halprin was touched by the beauty and mythical quality of Peter Brook's production *The Conference of the Birds*, appreciating the interaction between the performers, the quality of their physical and vocal work and the cross-cultural nature of his company (Halprin 2001b).

MOVING INTO THE COMMUNITY

The Watts project and *Ceremony of Us* (1968–9)

In 1968 a significant turning point in the evolution of the Dancers' Workshop occurred. Shortly after the Watts race riots in Los Angeles, Halprin was approached by James Woods, director of the Studio Watts School for the Arts, to create a performance for the Los Angeles Festival of Performing Arts. Woods had been impressed by the inclusive ethos of *Myths* and asked Halprin to create an event which would bring people from the black community in Watts into the prestigious Mark Taper Theater. Halprin, not satisfied to involve this community simply as an audience, worked regularly for several months with a self-selected group of young black people in Watts, and an equivalent group of white people in San Francisco. Halprin worked in similar ways with each group, developing movement resources and exploring personal, creative and group processes. Ten days before the performance the two groups were brought together. The encounter between them and the real and volatile process of the two groups learning to work creatively together became the raw material of *Ceremony of Us*. The performance focused on issues of power, sexuality, competition, aggression and ultimately co-operation and celebration. The issues that the performers were confronting were of vital importance to them, their personal investment was high and the touchstone of the performance was its authenticity. The audience had to choose whether to enter the theatre through a door where the black performers were assembled or another where the white group was gathered. The aim was to confront the audience with their racial attitudes from the beginning, involving them personally in the process of confrontation and reconciliation that the group had experienced. A final celebratory procession led the audience into the plaza outside the theatre where members of the public joined them. *Ceremony of Us* manifested Halprin's desire to create 'theatre where everything is experienced as if for the first time, a theatre of risk, spontaneity, exposure and intensity' (Halprin 1995: 101). It was a challenging process for Halprin, forcing her to confront her own attitudes and to engage with reality of cultural difference. The need for a method that could enable groups to work collectively across difference became apparent and precipitated the evolution of the RSVP Cycles for collective creativity (see Chapter 2).

As a result of the Watts project, the Dancers' Workshop transformed into a multi-racial group. The Reach Out programme, which received government funding for 12 years, was established to enable the participation of people from a cross-section of racial and cultural backgrounds, training them to become creative facilitators within their communities, and teachers and artists in their own right. Rather than superimpose white dance forms Halprin worked actively to develop the diverse movement resources of the group, for example black street dance, integrating them into the Dancers' Workshop programme.

Figure 1.5 *Ceremony of Us*, 1969, workshop. Photographer unknown, from Anna Halprin's personal archive

New Time Shuffle (1970), Kadosh (1971) and Moving Days (1973)

The Watts project was the Dancers' Workshop first confrontation with a major social issue. They continued to create work which engaged directly with contemporary social concerns working as a multi-racial group of 'performing social artists' in a variety of community locations (Halprin and others 1975: preface). In 1970 they performed *New Time Shuffle* a cabaret style performance at Soledad prison, a high-security goal known for it racial tensions. *Kadosh* (1971) challenged the relevance of Judaism and God in contemporary society at the time of the Vietnam War. Performed as part of the Friday night Shabbot service at a Jewish temple in Oakland, across the bay from San Francisco, *Kadosh* incorporated traditional Jewish texts and symbolic actions such as the lighting of candles and the tearing of garments. The Rabbi and the cantor actively participated in this dramatic and emotional interaction which expressed different attitudes to religious beliefs.

In 1973 the Dancers' Workshop worked with parents, teachers and pupils to create a score to return a school to its premises which had been rebuilt after being destroyed by fire. *Moving Days* combined practical tasks, such as moving the furniture, with symbolic gestures including ceremonial farewells to the school's temporary accommodation, a ritual invocation of the new building, and a celebratory procession, dancing and feasting. Such events rather than being participatory performances were collaborations with communities created with specific social intentions. The Dancers' Workshop had become more than a performance company. They saw themselves as a creative community whose personal, social and aesthetic values were intertwined, embodying a lifestyle rather than creating a dance style.

Initiations and Transformations (1971)

In 1971 following the trail blazed by *Ceremony of Us* the Dancers' Workshop created a new multi-racial performance work *Initiations and Transformations* which incorporated *Animal Ritual*, a score also performed in its own right. The animal imagery created a cohesive whole integrating the diversity of movement styles in the group and facilitated the expression of archetypal themes and interactions such as conflict, territory, attraction, isolation, family and hunting. In common with many of the other works Halprin created in this period, a cycle of conflict, catharsis, resolution and celebration occurred. Developed collectively the score for *Initiations and Transformations* was sufficiently open to allow each performer to create a new journey in response to it each time they performed, resulting in different versions of the work. The audience joined the performers in the final 'Trance Dance' which began with the group moving in unison to a repetitive drum beat. The intention was to create a 'moving community' with the company supporting the audience to claim ownership of the dance and create its own 'myth'. For Halprin this went beyond audience participation and was a genuine interaction between two communities (Pierce 1975: 13). Halprin understands trance dance as a collective process, an opportunity 'to experience . . . the journey from the self to the many and back to the self again'. In this context the 'myth' is a spontaneous 'event' which symbolizes 'the spirit of the collective psyche of the group'; it is unique, specific to that group at that time (Halprin 1995: 128).

At the American College Dance Festival in Connecticut in 1971 *Animal Ritual* was created by dancers from the Dancers' Workshop in collaboration with dance students at the festival through a process of parallel workshops similar to the one devised for the Watts project. Apparently unrepentant after her experience with *Parades and Changes*, Halprin returned to New York in 1971 and performed *Initiations and Transformations* with the Dancers' Workshop in the New York city centre. The use of nudity in this performance directly challenged taboos around sexuality and the body (Halprin 1995: 114).

Halprin's work and life experience during the 16 years that had passed since she had performed *The Prophetess* in New York at the Festival of American Dance in 1955 had so radically transformed her understanding of dance, her movement vocabulary and her approach to performance and creative process, that the images of her in *The Prophetess* and *Animal Ritual* are hard to reconcile.

Citydance (1976–7)

Citydance created in San Francisco in 1976 and 1977 was a synthesis of Halprin's experience creating participatory events in public spaces and working in a variety of urban and natural environments. Following the murder of San Francisco's mayor and another official (Amirrezvani 2000), *Citydance* aimed to regenerate a sense of community and an awareness of and revitalized connection to the urban environment.

Citydance (1977) was the culmination of a year-long programme of public events at the San Francisco Museum of Modern Art. A dawn to dusk journey through San Francisco, *Citydance* travelled through contrasting environments and neighbourhoods, including woodland, a ghetto playground, a skyscraper, a formal plaza in the city centre, a graveyard and the cable car terminus. The focus was on interacting with the environments, spaces and people of the city through simple scores which facilitated spontaneous expression and individual participation. Starting with a dawn ceremony looking out over the city, the event gathered momentum as it progressed with people joining along the way until the final exuberant celebration in the heart of the city with nearly a thousand participants. Halprin saw the journey in mythic terms; for her the group became 'a living embodiment of the city' (Halprin and San Francisco Dancers' Workshop 1977: 27). A celebration of community *Citydance* reflected the diversity of its participants, it included poetry, masks, face painting, a lunch ritual, an impromptu basketball game and an eclectic mix of live music, it began with a Native American chant and closed with bagpipes, African drumming and a Tibetan horn. All the participants in *Citydance* were considered 'co-creators'. Members of the Dancers' Workshop performed prepared pieces and guided the group process, participants who had attended the museum series had been involved in devising the scores, members of the public who had read the score in the local newspaper and passers-by joined in, others became unwitting performers. *Citydance* was the fruit of Halprin's developing practice in collective creativity and her continuing exploration of scoring for and facilitating large group events. The creation of *Citydance* laid the ground for the *Circle the Earth* series in the 1980s.

Citydances were also created by the Natural Dance Workshop in London (1977) and in Europe. This popular but little documented group, which operated in London from 1976 until 1980, was established by Jym MacRitchie and his partner Anna Wise. Originally a community artist from the Great Georges' Community Arts project in Liverpool, MacRitchie had worked with Halprin at the Dancers' Workshop in the early 1970s. The Natural Dance Workshop, operating concurrently with the burgeoning New Dance movement and the growth movement, offered a highly successful workshop programme open to everyone, which challenged elitist and stylized approaches to dance. The Natural Dance Theatre, their performance group, created

Figure 1.6 *Citydance*, San Francisco, 1976, 1977. Photographer unknown, from Anna Halprin's personal archive

large-scale participatory dance events and environmental performances. The Natural Dance Workshop introduced Halprin's approach to dance to the UK. Many of its students and teachers subsequently trained with Halprin and are currently working as independent dancers performing and teaching in universities and the wider community.

ENVIRONMENT WORK

THE COLLABORATIONS OF ANNA AND LAWRENCE HALPRIN

From their initial meetings and early study with teachers from the Bauhaus, the working lives of Anna and Lawrence Halprin have interwoven in a richly creative manner that both acknowledge as important to their development. A vital element within their work has been their reliance on observations of the natural environment as a consistent source of inspiration whether for dance or architecture. During the late 1960s their shared commitment to broadening participation in artistic projects with the resulting enrichment and reaffirmation of community was combined with a determination to establish processes to ease the difficulties inherent in such collective creative ventures. The RSVP Cycles, a structure that aids communication within artistic collaborations, was formulated by Lawrence Halprin during this period in response to his own needs as a landscape designer/architect and those experienced by Anna Halprin in her teaching and work with the San Francisco Dancers' Workshop. (See Chapter 2 for outline of the RSVP Cycles and Chapter 3 for application to a specific performance.) Together the Halprins worked on joint projects such as a series of summer workshops, 'Experiments in Environments', for architecture students and dancers from 1966 to 1969 (see Chapter 2) held in the city, at the Kentfield outdoor studio and at Sea Ranch where they had a house on the coast. This series proved mutually beneficial for architects and performers in generating creative material, while simultaneously allowing the Halprins to test out the fledgling framework that would become in its final form, the RSVP Cycles, an essential tool in their subsequent work. As a direct result of the workshop series the Sea Ranch Collective, a multinational group of performers and visual artists, was formed and continues to meet each autumn to extend their explorations of environment-based dance (Halprin and Sea Ranch Collective 2003).

SEA RANCH

While the outdoor dance deck at Kentfield had provided Anna Halprin with an unusual and inspiring place to work, of similar impact was the Halprins' retreat at Sea Ranch, a coastal community 100 miles north of San Francisco on the Pacific Ocean. The buildings were designed by Lawrence Halprin Associates (begun in 1962) to satisfy the needs of residents and to harmonize with an area of outstanding natural beauty. In the design process Lawrence Halprin used community participation and scoring to establish a series of guidelines that would ensure maximum blending of the buildings into the environment resulting in a major achievement in ecological planning. For Anna Halprin the house at Sea Ranch became a space for retreat and regeneration as well as providing an inspiring environment for the many summer workshops she taught there. The close proximity of Sea Ranch to the Pomo Native American settlement helped foster an ongoing interchange in which the Halprins were invited to ceremonies at the Pomo Roundhouse, along with colleagues and students on more public occasions. Anna Halprin reciprocated by welcoming members of the settlement to attend workshops or performance events that she had organized. The witnessing of each other's work and subsequent friendships proved influential in many aspects of Halprin's development as both artist and teacher.

WORK IN THE NATURAL ENVIRONMENT

Just as Halprin had refused to inhibit movement exploration by limiting what could be included under the term 'dance' or by controlling who could dance, similarly she expanded where dance could take place. The public face of this attitude was most in evidence in an urban environment with the San Francisco Dancers' Workshop events and performances such as *Citydance* and through their subversive use of conventional theatre spaces. However, the less visible, but nevertheless crucial, process of researching movement in nature has been a continuous thread throughout her career. Whether through intensive workshops, retreats and performance group research or as part of the Tamalpa training programme, the natural landscape has proved an inspirational force for Halprin and those working with her.

The underlying principles that guide her work in nature are based on three beliefs: that 'the human body is a microcosm of the earth', processes of nature offer aesthetic guidelines and nature is a healer (Halprin 1995: 214). Halprin emphasizes the physicality of response when working outside and the importance of heightening awareness through opening up the senses and 'isolating them so that you can focus on what's there' (Halprin 2001b). The multi-sensory approach and a sensuous, tactile engagement with places immediately undercuts the notion that the landscape might merely serve as an attractive backdrop for performance. Instead Halprin establishes a means of working *with* nature that integrates fascination with naturally occurring processes and patterns alongside personal and collective stories, images and emotions triggered by such encounters.

Although Halprin's work in nature forms an essential, abiding element of her teaching/research, it has little public visibility. Performances regularly take place within the workshop context, but the immediacy of personal response, the unpredictable nature of the elements and the inaccessibility of some sites militates against conventional theatrical performance. Alongside the more intimate workshop performance style in which the audience might more accurately be called witnesses, a body of work has developed in which Halprin works with filmmakers and photographers to give environmental work public artistic expression. *Embracing Earth, Dances with Nature* (1995), a video directed by Halprin and filmed by Ellison Hall and Andy Abrahams Wilson, is an example of such work. Halprin's work as a performer in *Still Dance*, created by performance artist Eeo Stubblefield, is discussed towards the end of this chapter.

CANCER AND THE HEALING POWER OF DANCE

In 1972 aged 51 Halprin was confronted by a personal crisis from which she emerged with a new sense of purpose. She had begun to use drawing (visualizations) to explore the relationship between imagery and movement. During a workshop she drew a grey ball in her pelvis that she felt unable to interpret in dance. On intuition she requested a medical examination of the area, which revealed a malignant tumour in her colon. Surgery left Halprin with a radically changed body (she had a colostomy) and with understandable concern about her future as a dancer. She was informed that if there was no recurrence of the cancer within five years she could consider herself clear. In 1975 the cancer recurred. Halprin, who had intensified her research into visualizations and movement after her diagnosis, fell back on her own resources. Recognizing that 'drastic changes' (Halprin 1995: 66) were needed she went into retreat and undertook an intensive emotional and physical exploration of her personal process through movement and drawing. As a result of this she created a personal ritual which effected a transformation in her healing process. She created two larger than life self-portraits, one an idealized image of herself as young and healthy and, on the reverse side, an angry and violent picture of her 'shadow' side. Supported by an intimate group of witnesses Halprin danced first the negative image releasing acute feelings of rage and pain and then her original portrait imagining herself being cleansed by mountain cascades flowing through her body. It was a powerful and emotional experience, a healing ritual that had a profound impact on her; her cancer went into remission and her priorities in her artistic work changed. Halprin felt that she needed to 're-evaluate my role as a dancer' (McMann Paludan 1995: 249); 'before I had cancer, I lived my life in service of dance, and after I had cancer, I danced in the service of life' (Halprin 2001a: 16). Theatrical performances slipped into the background as Halprin began to focus her attention on investigating the inter-relationship between art and personal process, the creation of dances which carried meaning for the individuals and groups involved, dances which had the power to effect change in people's lives.

In the last two decades of the twentieth century Halprin developed the use of dance and visualizations, now referred to as the Psychokinetic Visualization Process, with people facing life-threatening illness. She began to formalize the intuitive process she had used in her own healing, creating the Five Stages of Healing, discussed in more detail in Chapter 3. In 1980 she began to run workshops as part of a cancer support and education programme at the Creighton Health Institute in California. From 1986 she offered a cancer self-help programme entitled 'Moving Towards Life' at the Tamalpa Institute. In the mid-1980s Halprin was also invited to work with men and women living with HIV and AIDS which was fast becoming a major issue in the Bay area. This work led to the formation of the STEPS Theatre Company for People Challenging AIDS (which later became Positive Motion) and Women with Wings for Women Challenging AIDS through Dance and Ritual. Both groups continued for many years and performed in *Circle the Earth, Dancing with Life on the Line* (1989 and 1991), a large-scale performance ritual designed to address the issue of AIDS in the lives of individuals and the wider community (see Chapter 3). Halprin's book *Dance as a Healing Art* (2000) distills the knowledge gained through this 20 years of experience into a practical and accessible workbook. Her work embodies a holistic approach to the body and healing, reflecting the intrinsic relationship between the body, mind and emotions, integrating dance with feelings and images. Halprin expresses a deep-seated belief in the innate wisdom of the body and its power to heal itself, using dance as a means of empowerment, a way of 'reclaiming' a body in crisis and affirming the will to live (Halprin 1995: 207–8; Halprin 2000: 30).

TAMALPA INSTITUTE

Anna Halprin and Daria Halprin founded the Tamalpa Institute in 1978 as a response to the growing need to extend the training and research elements of the San Francisco Dancers' Workshop. The later Dancers' Workshop projects had become increasingly concerned with using dance and theatre to confront personal and social issues. This combined with community involvement and commitment to exploration of the healing purposes of dance were forceful reasons for focusing on the development of the Life/Art Process. The Tamalpa Institute was established to research the implications of this approach and 'to train others in a creative process which integrates psychology, body therapies and education with dance, art and drama' (Tamalpa Institute 1986a).

THE LIFE/ART PROCESS

The Life/Art Process lies at the heart of the workshop, training and performance work of the Tamalpa Institute. It was developed to investigate the complex and potentially transformative relationship between artistic expression and life experience. Key aspects of this method include a holistic approach to teaching dance, an acknowledgement of, and respect for, both differences and commonalties between people and a commitment to collective creativity. Although the political and philosophical implications of this path were not new in Halprin's work, as demonstrated by her community-based projects and Marin co-operatives, the performance aesthetic had become more precisely determined. There seemed to her to be little point in doing 'dances that were about being inventive and cute and funny when our planet is in such danger' (Halprin 1992: 53). In addition to the physical explorations Halprin had developed from her work with H'Doubler and Todd, she relied increasingly on methods such as the RSVP Cycles for collective creativity and the Five Stages of Healing (also known as the Five Part Process). The latter process was developed with Daria Halprin, who from childhood had worked with the Dancers' Workshop, subsequently training in Gestalt Therapy and developing her own approach to expressive arts therapy. The RSVP Cycles helped to make the different elements of the creative process visible and accessible, while the Five Stages of Healing encouraged participants to assimilate what they learned from performance back into daily life (see Chapter 2 for details). The application of this process to a community project that began as a series of workshops 'The Search for Living Myths and Rituals', and continues today as a yearly large scale ritual dance performance is examined in depth in Chapter 3. Tamalpa Institute students were closely involved with the project from its inception. Over the years it has shifted and altered form from the series of dances on the mountain that addressed an urgent local community issue, through to a flexible structure of workshops and performance called *Circle the Earth* designed to run in any country. As more people were inspired to create dance rituals in their own communities, in sympathy with the theme of peaceable living initiated in Marin, the worldwide *Planetary Dance* was created.

TRAINING PROGRAMMES AND PUBLIC EDUCATION

The Institute began to attract students from all over the world and from a range of fields including those engaged in the therapeutic, educational and caring professions as well as dancers, actors, musicians and visual artists. The Reach Out professional training programme, designed to foster a multi-racial student body, funded participants from countries and from sectors within America, such as the Native American population, who could not otherwise have afforded to participate. The intensive training programmes and the public education component (including community projects, summer workshops, public events, performances and publications) of Tamalpa have continued to reflect a holistic, inclusive approach to the teaching of dance. To this end the faculty offer a range of teaching skills, such as the physical awareness work of Moshe Feldenkrais, Gestalt work, active listening, collective creativity and environment work alongside the more traditional aspects of dance/theatre training. The training programmes vary year by year in response to the particular expertise brought by staff and guest artists, but the fundamental adherence to the Life/Art Process and belief in the potentiality of this to generate positive change in the individual and the community remains paramount. In 1991 Anna Halprin withdrew from the artistic management of the Institute but retained contact through teaching on specific programmes. The Tamalpa Institute continues to offer a range of training programmes and workshops under the artistic directorship of Daria Halprin and in the summer of 2003 celebrated its twenty-fifth anniversary with a special gathering of former graduates and contacts.

THE RELATIONSHIP WITH CONTEMPORARY DANCE

During the mid-1950s Halprin's shift away from modern styles of dance made popular by such choreographers as Martha Graham, Doris Humphrey and Hanya Holm, left her in an uneasy relationship with the dance world. This was not to resolve itself for many years and, during the early period of the Dancers' Workshop, Halprin's work was so misunderstood that she was accused of setting dance back 20 years (Kerner 1988: 12). However, the many elements of her work that made it incomprehensible to more conventional dancers and critics were the very attributes sought out by young avant-garde dancers. In the documentary film *Lawrence and Anna Halprin, Inner Landscapes*, dance scholar, Janice Ross, suggests that because Halprin 'always moved freely between the various art worlds. She was never locked in the pocket of dance only . . .' so instead of 'being stifled by it . . . she brought that very fluid stimulating environment to her work' (1991).

James Waring (1922–75), who was to make a name for himself as a dancer and choreographer in New York, had taught at the Halprin–Lathrop Studio, but Simone Forti (1935–) was the first dancer with whom Halprin spent an extended time after moving away from modern dance. Forti and her husband, the painter Robert Morris (1931–), shared the Halprins' interest in the history and philosophy of the Bauhaus with Forti noting the influence of the Bauhaus principles in the task-orientated improvisations that Halprin devised in their work together in 1955–9.

> The idea of these 'tasks' was to set up a structure or an object and to explore the physical possibilities that it offered. . . . in this way we were able to enrich our corporeal and kinetic imaginations directly – without recourse to external referents (literary or psychological) as had been the case up until then in most dance practices.
>
> (Forti 1999: 147)

As she worked with Halprin, Forti shifted from a primary interest in painting to dance. Both she and Morris welcomed the opportunity they found with Halprin of an extended period of experimentation with artists from a range of disciplines. In addition, Forti points to their openness to diverse influences, from Japanese performance, developments in visual art, use of collage/radical juxtaposition in performance and the practice of Zen Buddhism. 'We wanted to be open to the unknown, to welcome disorientation' (Forti 1999: 147). Forti took part in several of the early Dancers' Workshop performances such as the informal *Nez Plays* (Zen spelt backwards), *Four Square* (1959) and *Trunk Dance* (1959). Exploration of improvisation in performance and task-based movement experienced with Halprin, contributed to Forti's involvement with artists such as Allan Kaprow, Claes Oldenburg and musician La Monte Young in the creation of 'Happenings' when she moved to New York (Forti 1999: 149).

Forti and, to a lesser extent, Morris were responsible for increasing the interchange between the East and West Coast avant-garde performance artists that had begun with John Cage's and Merce Cunningham's visits to California. Cunningham was supportive of Halprin's initiatives, but he was already pursuing his own style of dance linked initially to experiments in chance combinations associated with composer John Cage. Although he visited Halprin and danced on the deck at Kentfield, their paths veered in different directions. He became more reliant on highly trained dancers and a distinct style of abstract dance based on the challenging execution of unusual combinations of movement sequences.

Forti took part in composer Robert Dunn's dance composition classes held at the Cunningham studio (in 1960–2). These developed into radical forms of improvisatory performance given in a series of concerts from 1962 to 1964 at Judson Church in New York (the groups of performers became known collectively as the Judson Dance Theater). It was Forti who suggested early on in this process that members of the class take part in Halprin's summer workshops in California. Subsequently in 1960 Yvonne Rainer (1934–) (choreographer, dancer and filmmaker) and Ruth Emerson (choreographer and dancer) went with Forti and Morris to Halprin's summer workshop where they worked alongside, amongst others, dancer and choreographer Trisha Brown, composer La Monte Young and actor John Graham. This proved to be a rich time for cross-fertilization of ideas between dance developing on the East and West Coasts of America. It had lasting implications for the Judson Dance Theater group of artists, including the subsequent solo development of well-known choreographers such as Yvonne Rainer, Trisha Brown (1936–) and later Meredith Monk (1942–). Dance scholar Sally Banes, in her book *Democracy's Body: Judson Dance Theater, 1962–1964*, suggests that Halprin's teaching provided members of the group with the 'freedom to follow intuition and

impulse in improvisation', experience of work in nature and an 'ana-
lytic approach to anatomy and kinesiology' (Banes 1993: xvii). Rainer
valued the freedom of the summer workshops where 'anything could
be explored and everything was up for grabs' (*Lawrence and Anna Halprin*
1991). While Monk found Halprin's 'affirmation to continue [her] own
path' important and suggests that 'maybe that's the beauty of the way
that she teaches and is as a person, that it really is an encouragement to
find your own way' (*Lawrence and Anna Halprin* 1991).

Over the years Halprin has been teaching, many dancers have been
drawn to work with her, while others like Forti, under her influence,
have changed course to become dancers. Her commitment 'to break
down the idea of separation between art and life' that Monk sees as
Halprin's mission (*Lawrence and Anna Halprin* 1991) is combined with
an openness to all art forms with the result that even artists connected
with specific styles of dance have found Halprin's material useful and
cite her influence as significant. For instance Cynthia Novack describes
the overlap of movement ideas and values in her analysis of the development of Contact Improvisation (Novack 1990: 29, 30). She selects
particular elements as influential such as the collective creative process,
development of structures for improvisation (scores), direct sensuous
experience of movement and an expanded range of movement rather
than a codified vocabulary (Novack 1990: 30).

While some well-known choreographers/dancers sought out Halprin's workshops or training programmes, for instance the British
choreographer Rosemary Butcher (1947–) and the American Mary
Fulkerson (1946–) who later taught extensively at Dartington College
in Devon, UK, others came across her work by chance. American
Deborah Hay (1941–) inadvertently took part in a Dancers' Workshop
performance called *Bath* (1967): 'A girl from the audience came into the
fountain and pressed her body against the statue' (Halprin 1995: 106).
While Kei Takei (1946–) (dancer and choreographer), who later
trained with Halprin, was an audience member for *Initiations and Transformations* (1972) and joined in the open section for audience members
with such energy and force that Halprin immediately noticed her presence. 'She just burst out of the "Trance Dance" we were doing and she
did a dance that was . . . she was just out of her mind' (Pierce 1975: 9).

The outdoor deck and studio at Kentfield has remained a meeting place
for artists to exchange ideas and methods of working even when styles
are apparently very different. For example although not particularly

drawn to the Japanese form of contemporary dance called Butoh (full name Ankoku Butoh – Dance of Total Darkness) which has become too rigidly codified for her taste, Halprin greatly appreciated the work of individual dancers who have worked closely with or within the Butoh style. When Min Tanaka (1945–) (renowned Butoh dancer/choreographer and founder of Body Weather), who originally met Halprin in Japan, visited her in Kentfield, the dances he performed on the deck confirmed in her view that he is 'a wonderful artist' (Halprin 2002a). More recently she has worked with dancers Eiko (1952–) and Koma (1948–), the Japanese couple who do not see their work as Butoh although they did train with Tatsumi Hijikata and Kazuo Ohno (known as the founders of Butoh). In 2001 they collaborated with Halprin on *Be With*, a dance that was performed in Washington, San Francisco and New York.

Movement-based theatre artists have continued to draw on Halprin's approach both for her methods of stimulating individual and collective creative response and for the structures that help formulate these into performance. For instance the French-Canadian theatre director Robert Lepage (1957–) was introduced to the RSVP Cycles through his work with Jacques Lessard, founder of Théâtre Répère. Using their own development of the process, 'resource, search, evaluation and presentation', the Répère method has contributed to Lepage's work with continuously evolving performances based, in part, on audience response.

DANCE AWARDS

Ironically after so many years of feeling more accepted by and in sympathy with the theatrical avant-garde, Halprin's achievements have gradually been acknowledged within the dance world with a series of awards. In 1980 during the twenty-fifth anniversary year of the San Francisco Dancers' Workshop she was awarded the American Dance Guild's Award in recognition of her work as one of the nation's leading exponents of experimental dance. While in 1994, aged 73, she returned to the University of Wisconsin to receive an Honorary Doctorate of Fine Arts. In 1997 she was presented with the Samuel H. Scripps/American Dance Festival Award, established in 1981 and one of the most prestigious dance honours for lifetime achievement, accompanied by a $25,000 cash award. The dedication Halprin received was a public, if belated, recognition of her extensive contributions to dance. 'Generations of dancers have been inspired by Anna, whose multi-faceted ideas have transcended traditional boundaries, embraced uncharted seas of expression and always encouraged freedom and the purity of unrestricted creativity' (Certificate 1997).

LATER WORK

80TH YEAR RETROSPECTIVE (2000)

In June 2000 The Dancers' Group, an organization which promotes dance in the Bay area, hosted an *80th Year Retrospective* for Anna Halprin at the Cowell Theater in San Francisco. The programme included extracts from *Parades and Changes*, *Memories from My Closet: Four Dance Stories* performed by Halprin, and the premiere of a new work, *Intensive Care, Reflections on Death and Dying*. It also featured a photographic exhibition *Still Dance*, the fruit of Halprin's ongoing collaboration as performer in the environment with performance and visual artist Eeo Stubblefield, a retrospective exhibition entitled 'Five Decades of Transformational Dance' and photographs of *Parades and Changes*.

Parades and Changes

From all her early works Halprin chose to recreate the 'Undressing and Dressing Dance' including the 'Paper Dance' from *Parades and Changes* for a number of reasons. The most important consideration was that she felt that the shocked reactions when it had first been performed in America in 1967 had prevented any real understanding of the dance. Her hope was that 30 years later an audience would be able to perceive it in the spirit in which it was created. She also felt that the dance had historical significance because it had challenged both the social and artistic norms of the era. In addition to the use of nudity the performance disregarded established gender stereotypes by dressing the performers androgynously and flew in the face of the conventions of contemporary dance by creating a work based on an everyday task. Pragmatically it was not a difficult dance to recreate as the movement vocabulary was easily accessible. In fact Halprin had previously reconstructed it with participants at the American Dance Festival in North Carolina in 1997, and at the Museum of Contemporary Art at Los Angeles in 1998.

Critical responses to the performance of *Parades and Changes* at the retrospective were enthusiastic. John Rockwell in the *New York Times* describes the 'Paper Dance' 'as striking a stage image as I have seen' comparing it to 'the best of the Living Theater, the Open Theater and early Robert Wilson' (2000). A clear contrast to the derisive 'no-pants dancers' headline in the same paper after the earlier performances (Halprin 1995: 6). The performance of these two scores from *Parades and Changes* is discussed in more depth in Chapter 2.

Memories from My Closet

The next section of the retrospective's programme was comprised of more recent works which are concerned with reminiscence. *Memories from My Closet* is a series of four dance vignettes inspired by memories associated with clothes and objects Halprin came across when clearing out her closet. The solos in *Memories from My Closet* are loosely strung together with the help of actor David Greenaway who combines the roles of master of ceremonies, interlocutor and costume assistant. The sequence commences with Halprin careering on stage in clown mode, complete with hat, large white shoes, a hat-box and a suitcase on wheels. Her entry is accompanied by a comic text spoken by Greenaway about her 'moving' career. Both the character and text are reminiscent of a much earlier phase of her performance work. All four pieces in *Memories* are created in an intimate story-telling style that includes direct address and combines movement and text. Halprin accomplishes the costume changes between the segments with pragmatism and panache, leavened by a mixture of comedy and self-parody.

The first piece *From 5–110* was inspired by a poem by James Broughton, a collaborator from the San Francisco Dancers' Workshop, for one of Halprin's birthdays. It follows Halprin's journey as a dancer from 5 to a putative 110 years old: through joyous childhood dances, adolescent rebellion and motherhood, to dances for peace and social justice, and now, at 80, dancing with a deepened understanding of the natural environment from the 'creepy crawlers' to the giant redwoods. Halprin envisages herself at 90 years old dancing as a healer and at a 100 dancing 'the essence of things', coming full circle to an exuberant childlike dance of freedom.

In contrast the *Courtesan and the Crone* is an unusually stylized performance for Halprin in which she transforms herself into a courtesan at the Venice Opera House. Donning an elaborate gown and evening gloves Halprin engages in a comic mock Italian exchange with Greenaway, remembering the performance of *Exposizione* at the Opera House in the early 1960s. A carnivalesque mask completes her transformation. In a highly theatrical performance, momentarily tinged with irony, Halprin masquerades as a much younger woman using a sequence of elegant hand gestures, flirtatiously displaying her legs and blowing kisses at the audience. The masquerade dissolves when she divests herself of her finery returning with deliberate and good-humoured bathos to the reality of her 80-year-old body. Unabashed she sends up the next costume change showing off her legs to the audience.

The Grandfather Dance mentioned at the beginning of this chapter is the third solo in *Memories from My Closet*. Performed to the music of a Jewish Klezmer band, this tender and exuberant celebration of her relationship with grandfather is the liveliest and most physically ambitious piece in the sequence and is danced by Halprin with verve.

Gratitude, the final vignette, is also the slightest. It is a personal ritual in which Halprin acknowledges her lineage. She performs in a Bedouin shepherd's robe which reminds her of her first visit to Israel in 1948 shortly after the establishment of the state, an experience which evoked a deep feeling of belonging and of homecoming. Naming her matrilineal and patrilineal ancestors Halprin scatters two piles of leaves across the stage with branches, using the symbolism of a tree to represent her forebears and all their descendents. In an attempt to bring her work with the natural environment into the theatre (Halprin 2001b) *Gratitude* is performed to the sound of bird song and the rustling of the leaves as Halprin runs through them and sweeps them across the stage. Unfortunately it has neither the theatricality nor the contact with the audience of the previous pieces and lacks the power of Halprin's performance work in the natural environment of which *Still Dance* is a striking testament.

Intensive Care

Premiered at the retrospective *Intensive Care, Reflections on Death and Dying* is a 40-minute investigation of our relationship with death. In this confronting work Halprin's intention is to marry an authentic exploration of the feelings around death with aesthetic considerations.

Halprin's motivation for creating *Intensive Care* interweaves a number of personal and artistic concerns. The immediate catalyst for the work was a period of two months in 1998 when Lawrence Halprin was unexpectedly confined to intensive care as the result of a simple surgical procedure going wrong. The dance also reflects Halprin's 20 years of work with people facing life-threatening illnesses, her own experience of cancer and an attempt to come to terms with her ageing process and the inevitability of death. *Intensive Care* was created in collaboration with three performers and was devised through an in-depth physical exploration of the feelings, associations and images which the theme of death provoked for each performer. Halprin views *Intensive Care* as a successful expression of the Life/Art Process; it combines a raw but crafted theatricality with intimacy and a rare degree of personal honesty.

Given the taboo nature of the subject matter, the emotional intensity of the performances and the raw nerves it touches, Halprin was uncertain about how *Intensive Care* would be received (Halprin 2001b). One critic confessed that 'it is not an easy piece to watch; and . . . it was not easy to turn away either' (Ulrich 2000); another described it as 'relentlessly compelling' (Howard 2000b). *Intensive Care* is discussed in more detail in Chapter 2.

Summing up

Halprin's *80th Year Retrospective* was enthusiastically received by audience and reviewers alike. According to John Rockwell of the *New York Times* the opening performance had an atmosphere of a reunion. While it is arguable that a significant proportion of the sellout audiences were people who had worked with Halprin over the years, both *Still Dance* and the performances themselves testified to Halprin's continuing power as an artist. Her natural performing presence, sense of theatrical timing and rapport with her audience, the range of work from comedy to the refined aesthetics of *Parades and Changes* and the emotional confrontation of *Intensive Care*, coupled with her physical expressiveness, demonstrate that in her eighties Halprin is still 'a moving force' (*Memories from My Closet, 80th Year Retrospective* 2000). Although Halprin professes that the retrospective was intended as a goodbye (Wolf 2000), she clearly had no intention of stopping dancing but rather in *From 5–110* prays for the time to dance all the dances which still remain. It is fitting for an artist who has consistently prioritized the ongoing evolution of her work over a definitive final product that Halprin's perspective in her *80th Year Retrospective* encompasses not only the past but is firmly rooted in the present and opens to a vision for the future.

RECENT COLLABORATIONS

Far from the *80th Year Retrospective* signalling an end to performance, in 2002 Halprin was back on the New York stage after several decades of absence. Included in the programme of dances at the Joyce Theater was Halprin's solo from the retrospective, *From 5–110,* Eiko and Koma's *Snow*, and a new collaborative piece, *Be With* (2001), with Halprin, Eiko and Koma and cellist, formerly of the Kronos Quartet, Joan Jeanrenaud. Demanding as it was to tour an extended programme at the age of 81, equally the processes undertaken in this and other recent collaborations testify to an undiminished desire to explore new ground. In *Be With* and the performance work with Eeo Stubblefield on *Still Dance*, issues of ageing, the role of the elder in society and awareness of death are to the fore, subject matter that many find uncomfortable, even taboo. While this for Halprin was a continuation of development of art from life experience, the making of the pieces raised a variety of very different challenges specific to each venture.

Be With (2001)

Be With, created by Halprin, Eiko and Koma, and Jeanrenaud, was commissioned by the Kennedy Center for Performing Arts in Washington and premiered there in October 2001. The Japanese couple, Eiko and Koma, have lived in New York since 1976, performing and choreographing their own dances. They have developed a style of 'movement theatre' that has been described as specializing 'in the art of elegy . . .' that operates in a 'world of infinite shadow and infinitesimally calibrated motion much of which is painstakingly slow' (Greskovic 1999: 99, 100). Although their work is frequently compared to Butoh, a contemporary form of Japanese dance, the couple resist this categorization. Halprin, however, noted several similarities in their work with the Butoh form (Halprin 2002a). Eiko and Koma 'have known and admired Anna Halprin from their earliest years in America, when they lived in California and took her workshops at the Tamalpa Institute' (Eiko and Koma 2002). For Halprin this was the first time she had created a public performance with dancers who had such a distinct style and creative method. This, combined with the challenge for Eiko and Koma of opening up their close working relationship to another dancer, made for a highly demanding process. To overcome these differences and to find a means of communicating successfully drawing on their respective backgrounds, they focused on specific themes emerging from their movement together. In particular they worked with the idea of journeying along a path by the studio wall and with the relationships that sprang out of the age difference between them (Halprin 81, Koma 53, Eiko 49). Gradually the piece began 'to take on a story just because of these external factors' (Halprin 2002a). As the devising process progressed Halprin found it easier to work with Eiko and Koma separately, since she continued to feel that when they danced together 'their style was so specific . . . there was no way into their world' (Halprin 2002a). It is possibly a repercussion of this that was noticed by Anna Kisselgoff in her review of the performance in New York: 'Eiko and Koma never dance directly with each other, rather, it is Ms. Halprin's personality that draws them in' (2002: 1). In the same review, however, she notes that: 'For all their differences, the three dancers share an interest in ritual and myth, an unself-conscious regard for the nude body and an affinity for nature' (Kisselgoff 2002: 3).

Inevitably part of the challenge of such collaboration stemmed from the issue of working across cultural difference. Halprin resisted the slow pace of the work particularly when the piece involved her in a section with Koma in which she had to assert herself forcefully. The slowness lacked authenticity for Halprin, denying the energy of the confronta-tion. Halprin recalls that Eiko's observation of that particular interaction was that it was more like a workshop than performance, thereby tapping into a criticism that has sporadically arisen during Halprin's career, that her performance is really therapy not art. In repudiating this view and refusing to maintain the slow pace which felt unreal for her, Halprin nevertheless took Eiko's criticism seriously and worked hard to refine the section, which, in performance, she felt Eiko came to appreciate (Halprin 2002a).

In the process of confronting deeply rooted differences in style, devising methods and aesthetic preferences Halprin suggests each of them had to make personal changes and adaptations (Halprin 2002a). The challenging process of creating *Be With* culminated in a demanding schedule of performances in Washington, California and New York. Reviewer Sarah Kaufman writes of the Washington performance that it was 'infused with undeniable beauty' and indicates the significance of Joan Jeanrenaud's contribution, 'the singing minimalist tones of the cello composition played on stage by its composer' (quoted in Yerna Buena Center for the Arts Theater 2002). While from New York, Kisselgoff notes the 'distancing effect of Ms Jeanrenaud's musicianship. She theatricalizes the activities, making them part of a performance rather than the usual Eiko and Koma dreamscape' (2002: 1).

Still Dance

Eeo Stubblefield, performance and visual artist, created *Still Dance* in 1981 as solo performance work arising from her response to chosen landscapes. She describes this work as weaving together 'performance, body art, story, photography and the particularity of a place' (2001). Initially she worked as performer, director and visual artist creating dance inspired by the quality or story of each place, with Peggy O'Neil taking photographs. The impetus of the danced exploration was towards the distillation of the dialogue between performer and place, rather than a conventional performance and it is this 'still point' (Stubblefield 2001) that lives on in the photograph. The body art and design elements are essential to each piece. They function on an overall aesthetic level, but, as significantly, support the integrity of the performer's experience (see Chapter 2 for details). Stubblefield's work with *Still Dance* had incorporated a wide range of people in the role of performer before Halprin began to perform with her in 1997. The outcome is a collection of photographs, which shows the collaborative work of artist/designer Stubblefield and performer Halprin in a variety of natural sites across North America. A body of this work has been brought together as an exhibition held in several venues and with each image described as 'the summation of a performance ritual, the arrival at the "still point" in which the voice of a living place is responded to by a performer' (Stubblefield 2001).

Stubblefield has a long connection with Halprin through the training programmes at Tamalpa Institute, as an artist contributing to *Circle the Earth* and *The Planetary Dance* and as a regular member of the Sea Ranch Collective. Facts that Halprin is quick to acknowledge as contributing towards the success of their collaborative work. In addition both

Stubblefield and later Andy Abrahams Wilson, who made the film *Returning Home* (2003) based on Halprin and Stubblefield's work with *Still Dance*, have a 'deep understanding of the kind of creative process' Halprin uses (Halprin 1997–2000) and a shared history of dancing with her.

The images of Halprin in each landscape are captivating, each one intensified by the design for place and body covering created by Stubblefield. Halprin's experience of the process is considered in detail in Chapter 2. Whereas Stubblefield's work concerned the story and the 'still point' within the performance ritual, Abrahams Wilson responded to the transitions between daily life, exploration and performance ritual. The film he produced traced the making of several of the *Still Dance* series, capturing both the poetic quality of this method of responding to the land along with the logistical challenges that were in store for Halprin as a performer in her seventies and eighties.

CURRENT WORK

The creative energy that has resulted in such an array of public perform-ance and continued teaching shows no sign of abating as Halprin embarks on directing an ambitious year-long project to mark each season. *Summer*, the first of the four sections of *Seasons* (2003) 'informed by the solstice theme of Emergence' (Halprin and Sea Ranch Collective 2003), once again broke new ground for Halprin. It was the first public performance given by the Sea Ranch Collective and the first time that her mountain home studio/theatre, deck and surrounding woods had been used for public performance. The day event, performed three times in June, took the form of a trail through the woods surrounding Halprin's studio with performances taking place in each of several sites plus a sensory workshop led by Halprin. At night, *Pathways*, described by one member of the group as a labyrinth dance (annotation to programme, Halprin and Sea Ranch Collective 2003), followed a dusk food ritual.

In her early eighties, Halprin rejects stereotypical ideas of ageing as 'retirement' from the world of work and instead embraces an altogether more robust attitude that values the elder in the community for their knowledge and experience built over many decades. Typical of her con-frontational approach to issues facing her, whether personal or social, she continues to employ the Life/Art Process to transform her own

Figure 1.7 *Seasons: Part One – Summer*, 2003. Photograph by Rick Chapman, San Francisco

observations of the ageing process into artistic expression. This involves a commitment to rigorous personal exploration through movement, not for purposes of retreat but as her current contribution to an equally energetic engagement with other artists and performers. As well as embarking on new projects such as *Seasons* she continues to mould and re-site past work in a recycling process that tracks the applicability of older performances/community rituals to current situations.

2

THEORY AND PRACTICE

INTRODUCTION

The visual and written documentation on Halprin's work from her early days as a modern dancer through to her current work is extensive. From the start of her career she has valued opportunities to share her views on dance in the public arena as demonstrated by the founding of *Impulse* magazine, through films, videos and the many contributions she has made to journals. In addition, her willingness to provide interviews, give presentations and document-specific projects has resulted in a sizeable body of work, some of which has been published and remains accessible. Evaluation of theoretical approaches to performance and of the performances themselves plays a vital role in her creative process, promoting a flexible, fluid attitude to both her theory and practice as opposed to reliance on a set style or formula. *Moving Toward Life: Five Decades of Transformational Dance*, the collection of writings compiled by Halprin with editor Rachel Kaplan and published in 1995, is the first time that such a wide range of documentation has been brought together in a single volume. It provides the reader with representative samples of writing and illustrations spanning her whole career. The text is divided into three broad sections: 'The Halprin Life/Art Process: Theory, History and Practice', 'The Work in Community' and 'Leaning into Ritual'. Each one is introduced and placed in context by dance writers Sally Banes and Janice Ross, with the editor Rachel Kaplan. These short essays help to establish the thematic underpinning of the structure of the book and relate this to relevant periods addressed.

The difficulty with such a collection is that not all the articles or interviews fit readily into the sections to which they are assigned, and, since the chronology is not always clearly signalled in the body of the text, some confusion for a newcomer to Halprin's work is inevitable. Given that several of the interviews included cover an extended period of Halprin's work, a degree of overlap and repetition is unavoidable. However, this is outweighed by the quality of content of the selections. Many of the articles were written contemporaneously with the events or practice they examine, with revisions and annotations by Halprin, or they are interviews with a particular thrust that open up specific debates about Halprin's work. In both cases they convey a sense of vibrant immediacy, a directness of approach combined with being highly informative. The style of the articles ranges from lively collo-quial interchanges between artists in which ideas seem to be formulated as they speak, to more formal records of methodological principles that have endured as foundational components in her creative process such as Movement Ritual, Psychokinetic Visualization, RSVP Cycles and the Five Stages of Healing. Throughout, the volume is richly illustrated with black and white photographs that capture moments of performance and workshops, while diagrams and visual scores elucidate the methods she has come to rely on that combine to make up the Life/Art Process.

The following chapter draws on those strands of the book that focus on her theoretical views on performance-making, supplemented by other sources when appropriate. Each section will address principles and attitudes governing major components of Halprin's work such as the body and movement, the Life/Art Process, shaping of creative mater-ial movement in nature and performance. Where appropriate, detailed analyses will be included of the application of these approaches to specific performances. More recent performances have been selected for this purpose to illustrate a richly productive period of Halprin's work. Halprin's shifts in viewpoint over time are indicated in each section together with the interweaving of different theoretical elements. Contemporary examples provide a lengthened perspective on a body of work that continues to evolve in response to the immediate challenges Halprin encounters.

BODY AND MOVEMENT

FORMATION OF PRINCIPLES AND VALUES

Halprin's disappointment in the modern dance she witnessed in 1955 propelled her into her own intensive research into movement. She could not accept that dancers should be so reliant on the aesthetic of the chore-ographer, that they train to mimic a single style, or that there was an ideal dancer's body. Exciting as modern dance developments had been, this was no time to close down on experimentation. To develop her own theoretical perspective on both the body of the dancer and move-ment itself Halprin returned to the basics. For her this meant drawing extensively on her student training with H'Doubler and ideas gained from Mabel Todd, combined with the Bauhaus workshop approach that valued the craft in each art form. Halprin undertook a systematic explor-ation of anatomy in order to understand the movement potential of each body part and the repercussions these movements would have on the whole body structure. She focused on physical tasks as initial stimulus for dance to bypass image, story or music as catalyst for creation, removing the possibility that dance could be seen as merely illustrative of other arts. Like H'Doubler, Halprin believes that the teaching of dance must address the integration of the physical, emotional, spiritual and intellectual aspects of each person rather than contribute to a dualistic split between mind and body. Unlike H'Doubler, however, Halprin's teaching looks beyond the aims of pedagogy and personal development through movement, to include communication in the public arena, whether in performance, ritual or community event.

During the early phase of improvisation, exploration and close observation of the children's classes she was teaching, Halprin began to consolidate views about the body and movement that were central to her work. These included recognition of the value of dance for everyone and a rejection of the exclusivity of certain dance forms. She empha-sized the importance of integrating the whole person in dance, resulting in content being driven by the dancer's own motivations and issues. She wanted to use the 'raw material of our lives to make our art' (Halprin 1995: xi). However, the early Dancers' Workshop improvi-sations based on the body itself became too introspective, in danger of replicating the very patterns and predictable repetitions she had wanted to abandon in her move away from modern dance techniques.

Collaborative work with artists of different disciplines allowed both a mutual cross-fertilization and a clearer understanding of the distinctive qualities and characteristics of dance, bringing renewed energy to improvisation. As actors, visual artists and musicians joined in the dance, more of the restrictions that had been inherent in modern dance fell away. The dancer could speak, sing, make sound, wear what they like or nothing at all, perform wherever they wanted and contribute directly to the creative process. By moving into 'explorations' rather than improvisation Halprin found the means to focus sharply on specific elements of movement rather than simply generating greater quantities of random material. Over decades of research, Halprin has created and refined tools to promote the pleasure of dance in a manner that is accessible for everyone. With application and determination these skills can be built upon to create 'a well-trained holistic dancer-performer' necessary for public performance of holistic theatre (Halprin 1995: xi).

THE KINAESTHETIC SENSE

Physical training alone is insufficient to develop the type of dance/ dancer that Halprin envisaged. Even if the starting point was an arbitrarily chosen movement, Halprin is clear that integration not separation is key, 'if you are aware of the feelings and sensations and images in that movement it will become dance' (Halprin 2001b). For teaching purposes Halprin isolates the physical elements for detailed exploration, to prevent overwhelming input that becomes hard to process. Halprin's focus on the kinaesthetic sense is not indicative of a conventional dance training that includes pressure to leave personal life at the door of the studio, nor a theatre instruction to work with an 'empty' or 'neutral' body. Instead, by drawing attention to this frequently ignored sense, she encourages both greater sensitivity to movement and a clearer idea of how this sense links to the others.

Linda Hartley, writing on body–mind centring, describes how movement is perceived 'not only through the vestibular nerves of the inner ear, but also through proprioceptive and kinesthetic nerves located in bones, joints, muscles, fascia and ligaments throughout the body, and through interoceptive nerves in the organs, glands, vessels, and nerves' (Hartley 1989: 28). The resultant flow of information allows the body to respond to external elements, to prepare for movement and to maintain a sense of positioning in space. An increased awareness of the kinaesthetic sense gives the dancer a greater sense of autonomy. In both her writing and teaching Halprin repeatedly stresses the aim of her work as enabling each individual to develop their own style of movement:

> Dance can be approached as a direct and natural way to move without any personalised aesthetics imposed from an outside authority. Dance is not necessarily graceful, pretty, or spectacular. Dance can be grotesque, ugly, clumsy, funny, frightening, and conflicted.
>
> (Halprin 2000: 23)

By advocating this broadened perspective on the nature of dance Halprin encourages freedom of exploration but not at the expense of discipline. She supports students to gain a sound knowledge of anatomy and the basic principles of movement in relation to space, time and force. Such an informed approach enables participants to gain confidence in assessing their physical ability and to take responsibility for growth. An example of the way in which Halprin applies detailed understanding of the physical structures of the body to the teaching of dance is evident in Movement Ritual. Shaped and reshaped over her career, Movement Rituals I–IV were created to support Halprin's own work and as a valuable teaching aid, with the heightening of kinaesthetic awareness at their core. They are in a constant state of evolution as Halprin continues to explore the potential of each movement sequence and adapt them for current requirements.

MOVEMENT RITUALS I–IV

Movement Ritual I, the most developed and fully documented of the rituals, consists of a series of movements starting from lying on the back and eventually coming to standing, in which 'every movement is organized around spinal action' (Halprin 1995: 37). It is designed to lengthen the spine and to increase flexibility and strength in order to extend 'range of movement, to release tension, and to maintain healthy tone in the body' (Halprin 1995: 37). While the movements themselves are not unusual and would be familiar to those who have experienced yoga, Feldenkrais or dance warm-ups, the specific qualities of Movement Ritual arise in the method of teaching, the flow from one movement to another, intention and suggested application. Halprin's terminology in describing the growth of the sequences is significant:

they sprang out of an urgent need 'to replenish my energy, restore my sensibilities, relax my mind and rest my body while in motion' (Halprin 1995: 45). The simple personal desires are readily understandable and momentarily mask the unusual aspect of the statement that she wishes to accomplish all this 'in motion'. Yet this throwaway phrase is key to her work since every aspect of it refers the listener, workshop participant, reader or observer back to movement. Essentially learning about the body and dance is experiential and even a lecture by Halprin is likely to have the audience experimenting with hand movements or up on their feet.

While she wishes for a similar 'feel good' result for those who learn Movement Ritual, she stresses that it consists of 'organized and structured movements rather than formalized or personalized patterns' (Halprin 1995: 45). Her emphasis is on 'the understanding that there are universal laws that do govern all movement' (Halprin 1995: 45). It would be just as valid for people to alter or create their own sequence based on the same principles, but more closely related to their own physical needs. This is consistent with Halprin's general assertion that: 'As a teacher or director of the group, I never told anybody what a movement should be or how it should look' (Halprin 1995: 77) Movement Ritual is taught through verbal instruction rather than demonstration. In conjunction with increased kinaesthetic awareness, the term 'ritual' reminds the participant that with regular practice, ideally at the same time each day, the sequence can enhance the understanding of how both internal (e.g. health, stress, age, energy) and external factors (e.g. environment, sound, temperature, light) impinge on movement ability.

The drawings (see Figure 4.2, p. 152) from the book on Movement Ritual I act as a reminder for participants of the sequence and show that it has been designed to flow readily from one movement to another in such a way as to release muscles that have just been worked and follow a progression from lying to standing. Although Halprin emphasizes that '[d]rawing towards or away from the spine is inherent in every movement' (Halprin 1995: 37); at the same time she stresses the value of the sequence in increased awareness of the pelvic region. Positioned at the centre of the body, the pelvis is essential to 'the balancing of the parts, mobilization of weight bearing, shifting directions and lifting' (Halprin 1995: 37). Halprin pays particular attention to the importance of the breath in Movement Ritual, alerting participants to the rhythmic cycle of breathing in three intervals and awareness of the diaphragm. The conscious linking of breathing with each movement is important 'to the physical efficiency of our movements and to our psychic behavior' (Halprin 1995: 36).

With little documentation on Movement Rituals II–IV these have remained fluid sequences described by Halprin as a four-part series.

> **Movement Ritual I** is performed primarily lying down.
>
> **Movement Ritual II** is performed standing up using falls, lifts, swings and balance.
>
> **Movement Ritual III** is performed moving through space – walks, runs crawls, leaps, and various ways of shifting weight.
>
> **Movement Ritual IV** is the variety of the possibilities of reapplying the elements in I, II and III in various combinations; there are as many combinations as there are people to discover them.
>
> (Halprin 1979: 12)

They can be used for the reasons above, as a warm up or as the initial stage in a movement exploration leading into devising scores for performance. Although the sequences are still performed with the purpose of heightening individual kinaesthetic awareness, as they become more energetic and encompass a greater use of space inevitably attention is broadened to include sharper focus on the relationship between the body and the impact of spatial, temporal and dynamic elements.

THE QUESTION OF TECHNIQUE AND 'DIRECT MOVEMENT'

When pressed by Nancy Stark Smith in 1987, Halprin agreed that it was possible to teach improvisation, through creating a stimulating environment within which to explore and by teaching 'people how to pay attention, how to listen to their body, to what's going on, to a kind of superlative awareness . . .' (Halprin 1995: 195). 'Direct movement', Halprin's preferred term, refers to her belief that 'each person really has their own style which is the result of combining using three levels of awareness [physical, mental and emotional] in relationship to intention' (Halprin 2001b). This can be nurtured and celebrated as expression of human diversity rather than mediated through the imposition of a set style. However, this does not imply absence of technique only that the technical aspects of her teaching are based on structures and principles that respect the autonomy of the individual. Halprin favours the use of the term 'craft' that encompasses a sense of acquiring skills, knowledge and experience in relation to the basic components of dance such as space, time, force, and gravity, inertia, momentum and rhythm. The technique lies in developing competence to isolate and move with each of these elements to determine movement quality. Awareness of this quality generates feeling states that contribute to the overall 'ability to experience yourself in movement' (Halprin 1995: 33).

Throughout her career Halprin has sought approaches to movement that support the dancer's spontaneity and individual expressiveness. Although willing to experiment with a wide range of techniques to further her understanding of the moving body, there are few that gain her full approval. For a period, Halprin underwent intensive treatment with Ida Rolf (1896–1979) and incorporated 'Rolfing' in the Dancers' Workshop training. This technique worked with deep physical manipulation of the connective tissue surrounding the muscles, allowing the body to find a balanced alignment in relation to gravity, resulting in increased vitality and greater freedom of movement. But Halprin felt that Rolf didn't always appreciate the emotional impact of her interventions (Halprin with Kaplan 1995: 84) and claims that Rolfing was not a significant influence on her work (Halprin 2001b).

Unlike Rolfing, which involved invasive and often painful manipulations, Feldenkrais' 'Awareness Through Movement' lessons offered a subtle and experiential approach to increasing body–mind awareness which encourage active participation. Norma Leistiko (1930–), a long-term member of the Dancers' Workshop, trained as a Feldenkrais practitioner. Through her teaching, the Feldenkrais Method® became an integral part of the Tamalpa Institute training programme and was used as a starting point for creative movement exploration. Halprin has remained appreciative of Feldenkrais' work saying recently that she 'never felt so at home in my body as I did working with Moshe's approach' (Halprin 2001c). The sense of familiarity she experienced doing his work was due in part to learning through self-discovery, but equally she shared with him a profound respect for the intrinsic grace and efficiency of the body in motion when freed of interference from fixed styles or acquired habits.

In addition to the focus on physical awareness, Halprin has developed a range of scores for pairs and groupings to extend experience of movement in relation to others. Whether through detailed pair work on active/passive roles and blending or large-scale, high-energy work based on shared imagery and everyday tasks, participants are encouraged to learn as much about movement through observation of others as through their own experience. The practical scores in Chapter 4 provide a fuller indication of the range of work Halprin includes in her continuing quest to understand the complex and intricate inter-relationship of the different aspects of the body. Although the tools she has developed to support the well-being and maximum expressiveness of the dancer continue to shift according to the needs of the moment, Halprin remains committed to equipping each participant with skills that allow confident exploration of the unexpected and unfamiliar. Direct movement implies an ability to move without recourse to habits or imposed style that can mask the feelings and motivations of the mover. Halprin looks to the body in motion as a constant source of inspiration for dance and, if treated with respect, a life-enhancing, energy-giving resource. How this primarily physical approach engages with emotional and imaginative material is addressed below, while later in the chapter the means of shaping physical explorations and performance are discussed.

THE LIFE/ART PROCESS

THREE LEVELS OF AWARENESS

The holistic nature of Halprin's practice means it is not possible to discuss her work from a purely kinaesthetic perspective. On the other hand, the kinaesthetic basis of her work, which at the simplest level utilizes sensation and the structure of the body as a starting point for movement, is in danger of being overlooked due to her emphasis on the inclusion of emotions, personal associations and imagery.

Halprin's approach is characterized by the integration of the three levels of awareness mentioned previously namely: physical (the body, sensory awareness, sensations, movement), emotional (feelings/emotions) and mental (imagery, associations, conscious reflection and integration into daily life). Halprin may focus on them individually in order 'to cultivate a larger range in each level of awareness' but ultimately she believes that the three cannot be separated (Halprin 2000: 28).

It is perhaps misleading to categorize movement simply as physical since dance is the key to, and provides the link between, all three levels of awareness revealing 'sensations, feelings, emotions and images that have long been buried in our bodies' (Halprin 2000: 30). It is the use of direct rather than stylized movement that enables this personal connection through dance. The 'technique' which Halprin hopes to impart to her students is an experiential understanding of the interconnection of the physical, emotional and associative levels of awareness (Halprin 2001b).

Spirituality is linked to the three levels of awareness and has periodically been presented as a fourth aspect of the equation. In San Francisco Dancers' Workshop and Tamalpa brochures of the 1980s it is related to ritual and universal principles (Halprin 1995: 15; Tamalpa Institute 1985/6). In *Dance as a Healing Art*, Halprin states that: 'It is the purpose of this work to integrate physical movement with feelings, emotions, personal images and spirit' (Halprin 2000: 20). In recent years Halprin tends not to separate out the 'spiritual' aspect of her work and resists attempts to define it, although she does relate spirituality to an experience of meaning which she sees as inherently human, referring to it as 'a sense of wholeness' (Halprin 2001b). From this perspective, an innate spirituality underlies most of her work although it is not allied to any formal belief system.

LIFE AND ART

The three levels of awareness are integral to the Life/Art Process which is the cornerstone of Halprin's practice. Since the mid-1960s, a period characterized by Halprin's growing interest in the ways in which art and life reflect and inform one another, coinciding with her involvement with the human potential movement, the creation of *Apartment 6* and her 'first serious training program' (Halprin 1995: 12), the interrelationship between life and art has been one of Halprin's major concerns. Halprin has referred to all the work prior to this time as a 'foundation', 'laying the groundwork to deal with real-life issues' (Halprin 1995: 12). The potential for Halprin's work to develop in this direction can be discerned as soon as she moved away from the stylization of modern dance. In the final performance of *Apartment 6*, the Dancers' Workshop achieved their intention to 'simply have two hours on stage of a real-life situation, in which you as a performer and you as a person were completely the same thing' (Halprin 1995: 99).

Further to Halprin's experience of cancer and the establishment of the Tamalpa Institute, the Life/Art Process became more clearly articulated. This process forms the basis of all of Halprin's artistic and teaching practice and combined with the Five Stages of Healing (explored in depth in Chapter 3) it is at the core of her work with dance and healing.

The Life/Art Process 'is based upon the principle that *as life experience deepens, personal art expression expands, and as art expression expands, life experiences deepen*' (Halprin 2000: 20). Far from art being divorced from life, the two feed each other. The boundary between them is permeable allowing a continuous process of interchange. Halprin's approach to movement helps participants to 'access the[ir] life story' and in turn their life story becomes 'the ground for creating art' (Halprin 2000: 20). This may include creating performance scores based on significant relationships, incidents or issues in one's life. The value of the artistic experience is derived from the meaning it holds for participants who are encouraged to integrate any insights gained into their lives.

The Life/Art Process operates on a group and community level as well as individually. Since the Watts project in 1969 Halprin has continued to address social and community issues through her workshops and performances. Personal issues are contextualized within the collective experience. In some projects this has been intensified through groups living and working collectively. In *Carry Me Home*, a performance created by Positive Motion in 1990, Halprin used the Life/Art Process with a group of men dealing with HIV/AIDS to address issues which were both personal and collective. The performance was inspired by one of the members saying goodbye to the group before returning home to die.

For some years after her cancer, Halprin was primarily preoccupied by the ways in which the art process could be used to enrich people's lives, and aesthetic considerations became less important (Halprin 2001b). In her later years Halprin has looked for balance between the two terms of the Life/Art equation. Her criterion for teaching is to provide her students with an experience of the Life/Art Process which is coupled with a clear recognition of the value of craftsmanship (Halprin 2001b). In her performance *Intensive Care* (2000), discussed later in this chapter, the integration between life and art is powerfully manifested.

THERAPEUTIC APPROACHES

Halprin has explored a variety of therapeutic approaches in the development of the Life/Art Process. The most enduring therapeutic influence on her work with personal process is Gestalt Therapy as discussed in Chapter 1. However, bio-energetic body therapy based on the work of Wilhelm Reich (1897–1957), the most well-known exponent of which is Alexander Lowen (1910–   ), was also a significant influence. The underlying principle behind bio-energetic therapy is that repressed emotions, memories and trauma are held in the musculature of the body (described as armour) causing restrictions to both physical and emotional functioning. These emotions may be accessed directly through the body, for example by using stress positions which challenge habitual holding patterns. When the physical holding is released the emotions locked within it are also released through catharsis, and increased energy becomes available. Working in collaboration with therapist Dr John Rinn, whom she had met through Perls, Halprin devised bodywork exercises inspired by bio-energetics. These exercises were designed to break through physical limitations and emotional control in order to extend the physical and emotional range available to participants artistically. The exercises deliberated provoked intense feelings such as aggression and sexuality allowing the participants to access previously repressed material which could then be transformed creatively. This process provided Halprin with a necessary safety valve for potentially dangerous feelings such as violence and a means to enable participants to work safely and consciously with volatile emotions in performance. Although Halprin no longer works directly with bio-energetics, the underlying principles continue to inform her work.

Gestalt Therapy and bio-energetics provided Halprin with a broad understanding of the 'feedback process between movement and feelings' (Halprin 2000: 24). How you feel influences the way you move, and conversely certain ways of moving are likely to engender certain feelings. Movement is therefore capable of both expressing and transforming your emotional condition. Broadening your personal movement vocabulary allows you to experience, express and integrate a wider spectrum of emotions in daily life, enabling you to move beyond habitual limitations (Halprin 2000: 25). The application of this 'feedback process' to dance is central to Halprin's work.

Alongside these confrontational therapeutic techniques Halprin used 'active listening' to enhance communication and resolve conflict between individuals and within the group. Inspired by the client-centred therapy of Carl Rogers (1902–87), active listening was developed by Thomas Gordon as a tool for effective communication which aims to engender understanding of differing points of view. Working in pairs, one person speaks about their feelings or experiences of a particular issue while their partner attempts to reflect back the information communicated without judgement or interpretation. This non-judgemental attitude which validates the individual's experience, is fundamental to Halprin's practice. She has also applied 'the principles of active listening' to 'partner work in movement' and to the concept of witnessing a function which she subsequently extended to include the audience (Halprin 1995: 125–6).

PSYCHOKINETIC VISUALIZATIONS

Imagery plays a key role in the Life/Art Process. Combining dance and visual images was a natural development of Halprin's interest in the interaction between art forms. She began to incorporate drawing in her early work with children as a means of engendering creativity and a way of helping them to appreciate their dances. As her work developed drawing offered a way of exploring the connection between the body and the mind (Halprin 1995: 65).

For adults, drawing their dances validates and externalizes an ephemeral subjective experience and offers a means of reflecting on that experience which bypasses intellectual analysis. Initially Halprin turned to drawing as a way of working creatively with feelings that were overwhelming participants, creating an impasse in the creative process (Halprin 1995: 196). As her approach evolved they provided a way of integrating emotional material consciously. The interplay between drawing and dancing offers the individual the opportunity to reflect on the meaning that the movement holds for them and how it relates to their 'personal mythology' (Halprin 2001c).

Halprin works with 'visualizations' in different ways. 'Guided visualizations' are used to lead participants through an imagined experience while in a state of relaxation (Halprin 2000: 73). Halprin frequently uses natural images, an environment, an animal or an element, which she may locate in the body, followed by a movement exploration of the image. She has found guided visualizations particularly helpful when working with people in pain as a means to facilitate 'a connection to the body through a more spiritual dimension', reminding people of their connection with nature and 'our innate relationship to the larger life force' (Halprin 2000: 129–30).

Drawings of personal images, or 'visualizations', become known as 'Psychokinetic Visualizations' when the images are connected to 'movements and feelings/emotions through dance' (Halprin 2000: 26). The process may start with the participant imagining an image which they draw freely (artistic merit is not a criteria, the power of the drawings is derived from their personal content); the visualization is then 'danced' (Halprin 2000: 28). Equally a visualization may express the images, sensations and feelings evoked during a dance. The process is ongoing with one cycle of moving and drawing leading to another. Words or phrases may be added to a drawing and then vocalized or reinterpreted through chants, song, stories or poems. They may be used to highlight the physical, emotional and imaginative aspects of the drawing relating it to the three levels of awareness. Creative and journal writing are also used as a way of revealing more about the images and their connection to daily life. Halprin has not discovered any system of codifying the meaning of particular images but claims that the personal content of an image becomes apparent through the process of Psychokinetic Visualization. She notes that certain images recur but rather than interpreting these archetypally she feels they indicate the interrelatedness between human beings and our shared environment (Halprin 1995: 66).

For Halprin this process of working with Psychokinetic Visualizations allows participants to tap into unconscious imagery and knowledge: 'an intelligence within the body . . . deeper and more unpredictable than anything I could understand through rational thought' (Halprin 1995: 65). This is demonstrated dramatically through her experiences working with self-portraits.

SELF-PORTRAITS

The role that visualizations and self-portraits played in the diagnosis and remission of Halprin's cancer has already been discussed in Chapter 1. Self-portraits have been a central component of Halprin's training programmes since before the Tamalpa Institute was founded and they continue to be an important element of her work. These portraits, frequently life-size or larger, are the culmination of an intensive process linking physical explorations to emotional life scripting and images associated with different parts of the body. They also become the score for solo performances. In the Tamalpa training, self-portrait dances have become a rite of passage for generations of students. The way of creating self-portraits has varied over time and according to the situation. Sometimes an outline of the body has been drawn and filled in as different areas are explored; each body part may be drawn in turn until the portrait is complete; or the portrait is drawn in its entirety at the end of the process. Smaller drawings of each area will have been made throughout. Significant relationships and the environment may be included in subsequent self-portraits. In shorter workshops or presentations Halprin may focus on one part of the body through physical exploration and visualizations. She frequently uses before and after portraits to externalize changes that may have taken place during a workshop process.

Halprin's experiences have left her with a healthy respect for the power and mystery of working with self-portraits. On more than one occasion a self-portrait has appeared to prefigure an event which has subsequently happened. Notably Lawrence Washington's self-portrait in 1970 which seemed like a premonition of a fight in which he became seriously injured. Washington only began to show signs of recovery from the resulting paralysis in his limbs when at his request Halprin symbolically cut the chains which bound them in his portrait (Halprin 1995: 126). The implication is that visualizations may not only reflect a layer of reality of which we are not consciously aware but may also create that reality. For this reason Halprin insists that all elements of a self-portrait are fully explored through dance, if necessary magnifying particular areas of the image in order to unlock their significance. She compares this process to the Gestalt technique of embodying every element in a dream in order to understand its meaning (Halprin 2001c).

The use of guided imagery in the holistic treatment of illnesses such as cancer is now widely acknowledged. Halprin's work in translating such images into dance takes this process a stage further. It seems a logical development to embody these visualizations if one is intending to support physiological change. In her work with people with life-threatening illnesses, Halprin suggests that they visualize a cell in their immune system that is capable of overcoming their illness. She encourages them to draw it in as much detail as possible, then dance the visualizations and apply the knowledge gained when dealing with their illness in daily life (Halprin 2000: 112–13). In her self-portrait dance while struggling with cancer Halprin describes not only a physical and emotional catharsis but a healing experience of an altered state.

There is a sequel to Lawrence Washington's story which provides a dramatic illustration of Halprin's application of the Life/Art Process. A year after his recovery Washington had a seizure during a performance of *Animal Ritual* in New York. Honouring a prior agreement to respond to such an occurrence through the medium of the performance Halprin embodied a mother deer giving birth and nurtured Washington back into movement. When questioned about this experience it is clear that for Halprin at that moment there was no distinction in her conscious-ness between the real-life situation and her artistic response to it, which is perhaps why her strategy proved so effective. Not only did Washington recover enough to continue with the performance but the audience were unaware of the occurrence (Halprin 2001b).

SHAPING THE CREATIVE PROCESS

THE NEED FOR STRUCTURE

The radical experimentation in which Halprin and her artist collabora-tors engaged during the 1950s and 1960s yielded performance and workshop material that defied the conventional limitations associated with both the dance and theatre of the period. However, alongside the dynamic, dramatic possibilities this work entailed, compelling questions arose concerning issues stimulated by the artists' innovative methods. Paradoxically the opening of certain boundaries created new limitations and impasses based on recurrent patterns of movement that seemed to lead nowhere. Halprin expressed concern that however useful improvisation might be in generating material, there was an inherent danger in repeatedly going 'up to a certain point' and then just leaving it to 'go to something else' (Halprin 1995: 192). The greater discipline demanded by pursuing what Halprin terms 'dance explorations' ad-dressed this issue through ensuring specific focus on, for instance, a single element of time, space or force. This in turn would generate information that she later 'began to call "resources"' (Halprin 1995: 191). Although 'exploring was much more focused and more controlled than "improvising"' (Halprin 1995: 191) and had developmental possi-bilities, there remained difficulties in finding a form for the work.

In order to solve this and find a workable method of shaping creative material she worked with Lawrence Halprin on scoring:

> It wasn't enough to have a momentary movement image feeling. What do you do with it? Where does it go? And that's when scoring came in, which opened a lot of new creative possibilities. That was the most freeing most liberating experience of my life.

(Halprin 1995: 198)

From interviews and writings it is apparent that the development of a more systemized approach took place gradually. For instance there is evidence early in the 1960s of initial use of such elements as scoring and resources that would later be incorporated into the system for collective creativity known as RSVP Cycles. From the outset scores took many forms ranging from succinct lists of instructions, through primarily pictorial mapping of a performance, to elaborate use of grids and symbols to allow large numbers of participants to work simultaneously on varying pathways. However intricate or aesthetically pleasing the design, the function of scores was to convey essential instructions along with a theme and/or intention for the performance. Ideally the score would be sufficient to stimulate performance, although in practice some additional verbal direction might be necessary. Scores reflected the diversity of purpose as much in form as in content, whether required for community performance, ritual, self-portraits, solos, workshops or public dance performance (see Chapter 4 for examples).

A further issue that pressed for resolution during the early stages of Dancers' Workshop performances was the need for effective means of communicating when committed, as Halprin increasingly was, to collective creativity. During Halprin's work on *Myths* (1967–8), participatory events that encouraged the blurring of performer/audience roles, she began to value a fresh definition of the artist, as 'a guide who works to evoke the art within us all' (Halprin 1995: 131). This shift in emphasis required a clearly structured means by which participants and 'guides' could communicate and build on the creative material released.

For some time Halprin had observed the use of a variety of methods of scoring employed by avant-garde musicians such as John Cage and Morton Subotnik, including the use of chance, and Subotnik's 'cell-block' scores that were used in the Dancers' Workshop performance of *Parades and Changes* (1965–7). However, Halprin states: 'It still hadn't sunk in to me that *I* could use scores until I began working with my husband and he began to evolve this system of open to closed scores' (Halprin 1995: 200). Lawrence Halprin confirms that he 'first started on the RSVP Cycles as a design tool. Not so much for myself, but for my wife, Anna' (Halprin, L. 1999: 50). The value of the scoring process that Lawrence Halprin designed initially is illustrated by its effective use by Anna Halprin in Stockholm in 1966. She had taken *Parades and Changes* to Sweden but encountered difficulties in explaining the tasks necessary for the performance to the Swedish participants. Lawrence Halprin devised a score for them which 'worked. They could follow the score' (Halprin, L. 1999: 50).

Halprin's commitment to making dance accessible, validated by the success of *Myths*, created an urgent need to solve communication problems. *Ceremony of Us* (1969), the cross-cultural project undertaken in Watts, Los Angeles and San Francisco, proved a crucial point in Halprin's growing need for a flexible system that would facilitate ease of communication across social, racial and cultural differences during the collective creative process:

> Our ways of speaking, and our language and our images were so different we weren't hearing each other. We didn't know how. So we developed this RSVP Cycles so that we could listen to each other and find a way to respect our differences and find our commonality.
>
> (Halprin 1995: 17)

DEVELOPMENT OF SCORING

Prior to the development of the RSVP Cycles that encompassed the whole of the creative process, the Halprins worked together on the development of one of the elements: scoring. 'Experiments in Environment' was the first of a series of summer workshops for architects and dancers that took place between 1966 and 1969. Organized by Anna and Lawrence Halprin, it is illustrative of their joint work on a scoring process that could address the issues outlined above. In this instance the communication difficulties were compounded by the cross-arts nature of the project. The processes they, and other workshop leaders, developed had to be sufficiently open to support experiential learning while retaining clear focus. As her experience of multimedia performance increased, Anna Halprin was concerned that, without due care, cross-art collaborations could become superficial, with 'each artist going his own way and the composition instead of increasing the potentialities of theatre, grows cluttered and confused' (Anderson 1966: 54).

During the same period Lawrence Halprin wished to impress on his students the necessity of designing with a high degree of sensitivity to both urban and natural environments and in direct response to community requirements. He therefore

> welcomed the opportunity of having his students work with dancers in specific city and country sites because it would take the young architect away from the world of the drawing-board into the real world and force him to deal directly with structures in space.
>
> (Anderson 1966: 54)

In the first 'Experiments in Environment' summer workshop (1966) the Halprins and other workshop leaders (including sculptor Charles Ross, lighting designer Patric Hickey and actor Norma Leistiko) worked with up to 50 participants divided into two groups. In one group Lawrence Halprin had recruited young architects who worked on heightening their awareness of the impact of the city's architecture in downtown San Francisco. The movement classes they took actively encouraged them to make use of their architectural skills in understanding the structures of the human body. In 'one class, they used their own bodies as human cantilevers to build groups which choreographers might hesitate to create, but which, thanks to their knowledge of architecture transferred to dance, were anatomically safe and sound' (Anderson 1966: 56).

The second group, who were primarily young students interested in dance but not necessarily from a conventional dance background, spent time developing their awareness of their own movement capacities while gradually developing their physical range and creative response to the variety of stimuli presented to them. These included explorations of architectural problems such as being instructed to 'investigate energy in relation to gravitational pull . . .' which resulted in a theatre event 'held at dusk, in which people and objects were sent up and down the slope in varying ways. Like falling stars winking flashlights zipped along on pulleys' (Anderson 1966: 56).

Throughout the intensive month of work, as well as learning to grapple with each other's art medium alongside their own, the participants experienced collective projects often based on simple instructions,

Figure 2.1 Workshop at the ocean, summer 1966. Photograph by Paul Ryan

including scoring, designed to stimulate a creative response rather than a controlled outcome. For example, at Sea Ranch all 50 participants were directed by Lawrence Halprin to build a structure for themselves from the driftwood on the beach, without talking to each other and staying within a 150 foot radius of the centre where he had placed a stick. Anna Halprin recalls that whether the participants worked in pairs, alone or in groups: 'In each instance a unique statement evolved – a personal and imaginative driftwood structure' (Kostelanetz 1970: 76). Without planning, connections were made between the structures until after only three hours a driftwood city had been built 'with a gate, a main plaza, a temple, a tower, a stage structure in the water, and houses' (Burns 1967: 135).

Over subsequent summer workshops the Halprins, together with other facilitators and participants, refined the scores in response to initial results and new demands. For example, communication difficulties encountered during the creation of *Ceremony of Us* determined the focus of the 1969 summer workshop that included participants from Studio Watts in Los Angeles and a wide range of neighbourhood centres and colleges in the Bay area. 'We were black/white; rich/poor; Ivy League education to ghetto streets; the mystic drug-oriented hippie to the hardcore realist' (San Francisco Dancers' Workshop *c.*1970/1: 7). Drawing on scoring together with the fledgling system of the RSVP Cycles, participants experienced 'a painful struggle for survival as well as joyful celebrations' as they discovered 'new ways to meet the staggering challenge of differences that [a]ffect us all' (San Francisco Dancers' Work-shop *c.*1970/1: 7). Many of those involved became the basis of a long-lasting group that met regularly at Sea Ranch each summer.

The experimental work in the summer workshops was significant in the development of the principles of Anna Halprin's subsequent work, including the integration of emotional material in creative work (supported by workshop leaders such as therapist John Rinn and psychologist Dr Paul Baum), the use of the Life/Art Process and the significance of art expression for communities. The instant performances created in the city, on the dance deck and at Sea Ranch using task-based scores and props such as cargo nets, scaffolding and rolls of paper, filtered back into public performances and projects by the Dancers' Workshop. For example the City-Map score (1968) was a prototype for *Citydance* (1977). However, the difficulties of establishing clear communication across differences essential in the process-orientated work the Halprins espoused required a framework to encourage maximum individual participation while retaining clarity of group intention. Although the scores given to participants had generated fruitful work, they focused primarily on one element of the collective creative process, the instructions. In response to the application of scoring techniques with Anna Halprin and through further research in preparation for his book on scores, Lawrence Halprin gradually began to situate the scoring process within a wider framework that addressed what he regarded as the other essential components of the collective creative process.

RSVP CYCLES

Lawrence Halprin's interest in the use of scores, ranging from calendars to musical and ecological scores, grew from two sources. First

> because I am professionally an environmental designer and planner involved in the broad landscape where human beings and nature interface; and second because of my close relationship to dance and theatre due largely to my wife, the dancer and choreographer Ann Halprin . . . .

> (Halprin, L. 1969: 1)

As well as wanting to find a method of communication to facilitate non-goal-orientated creative process, he also wished to find the 'means to describe and evoke processes on other than a simple random basis' (Halprin, L. 1969: 1). Gradually, as he located elements that were not part of the scoring process, he found that his project had extended from being a book on scores to covering the whole creative process. He formulated this into four closely related sections defined as:

R Resources are what you have to work with. These include human and physical resources *and* their motivation and aims.

S Scores describe the process leading to the performance.

V Valuaction analyzes the results of action and possible selectivity and decisions. The term 'valuaction' is one coined to suggest the action-orientated as well as the decision-oriented aspects of V in the cycle.

P Performance is the resultant of scores and is the 'style' of the process.

> (Halprin, L. 1969: 2)

The term 'Performance' is used broadly to refer to putting the score into action and therefore includes 'performances' taking place during workshops, rituals and rehearsals as well as theatrical performance for an audience. There is no prescribed order for the different elements of the process so that it is adaptable to a wide variety of situations with overlaps and flows in different directions encouraged. For instance, valuaction of a performance might result in new resources, changes to the score or simply reperforming the original score. The Halprins emphasized that in any group creative endeavour there are always two cycles in operation: 'the cycle must work at two levels . . . The private, self-oriented inner cycle and the community group-oriented outer cycle' (Halprin, L. 1969: 3).

While the appeal of the system lies in its clarity and communicability, the apparent simplicity of the structure conceals the deeply held political principles that underlie it. Lawrence Halprin points to the importance of making the procedures of the creative process visible: 'In a process-orientated society they must all be visible continuously, in order to work so as to avoid secrecy and the manipulation of people' (Halprin, L. 1969: 2). A point reiterated by Anna Halprin who distinguishes it from other methods of working collectively: 'RSVP Cycles differ in that they systematize and make visible the whole creative process *as* it is occurring' (Halprin 1995: 48). She sums up the impact the method has had and continues to have on her work in the following way:

> The RSVP Cycles are the most important set of principles I have worked with because they extend and formalize a method of applied democracy. We have been able to explore attitudes, feelings, and personal objectives which are in themselves very subjective and which can be objectified in this form. The RSVP Cycles give people a sense of commitment, responsibility, and self-determination, encouraging them to take part in whatever it is that affects them.
>
> (Halprin 1995: 46)

These values inherent in the system will be examined in more detail in Chapter 3 through an analysis of how the process was applied to Halprin's large-scale performance series, *Circle the Earth*.

OPEN AND CLOSED SCORING

The use of scores in Halprin's work can be seen as a further refinement in her move away from open improvisation towards the more sharply focused 'explorations' mentioned earlier. Aided by Lawrence Halprin's formulation of scoring systems she began to locate scores on a scale from 1, representing open, to 10, representing closed. An open score contains a minimum of instructions leaving the participant free to explore, while a closed score consists of detailed, precise directions predetermining much of the action and severely limiting the freedom of the participant. In teaching scoring at Tamalpa, Halprin recommended aiming for about 5 on the scale to ensure sufficient stimulus and focus for performers while retaining a reasonable degree of space for individual creative response. However, as illustrated in Chapter 3, scores at either end of the scale have their own distinct functions and Halprin uses almost the full range when appropriate in her teaching and performance.

While the flexible scoring process of the RSVP Cycles became crucial in the creation and shaping of performance, it operates in conjunction with other important processes such as the Five Stages of Healing (also known as the Five Part Process), the Life/Art Process, active listening and Psychokinetic Visualizations. The score provides a sufficiently clear and secure framework to allow for exploration of the unknown to take place even in public performance. The resulting immediacy for both performer and audience emerges from a system that lessens the distinction between process and goal, viewing both as part of a continuum that feeds back into future performance and, as importantly for Halprin, into each participant's own life.

PERFORMANCE

OVERVIEW

The outline in Chapter 1 traces Halprin's evolving relationship to performance during her years with the San Francisco Dancers' Workshop and in her subsequent work. A journey which has led her further and further away from traditional notions of, and venues for, performance. In 1989 Halprin described herself as 'at heart, . . . a theater artist' (Halprin 1995: 24). Despite the physical basis of her work Halprin feels more at home with theatre than dance because of theatre's capacity to include emotional content which dancers frequently shy away from, dismissing it as 'therapy' rather than a valid dimension of dance practice (Halprin 1995: 245).

Speaking of her work in the 1960s and early 1970s, Halprin describes herself as an 'adventurer' who wanted to break free from 'confining rules' (Halprin 1995: 206). In the process she questioned the parameters of contemporary dance challenging the hegemony of the prevailing dance styles, the content and function of dance and a narrowly defined understanding of the dancer's role, and also pushed back the boundaries of performance itself. Rejecting conventional structures of performance Halprin increasingly created work in non-theatre environments, collapsing the boundaries between art forms and disrupting the relationship between performer and audience.

Her trajectory seemed propelled by its own energy. Early experiments with improvisation and anatomical explorations gave way to the development of task-based movement and increasingly integrated cross-artform collaborations. Words, voice, objects and environments were incorporated into her dance works, which were created collaboratively and frequently structured through the use of complex and flexible scores. Authenticity increasingly became the touchstone of Halprin's aesthetic as daily life situations and personal psychological material were introduced into performance.

As a precursor to expanding her work beyond the confines of theatre buildings Halprin's performers claimed the whole theatre environment as their performance space invading the previously protected territory of the audience. The energetic reactions of audiences to Halprin's iconoclastic experiments became a 'driving force' (Halprin 1995: 8) in the development of her work as Halprin began to involve them directly in the artistic process. The San Francisco Dancers' Workshop had initially taken to the streets to perform as a pragmatic solution to a shortage of funds and performance venues and as a source of 'ready-made audiences' (Halprin 1995: 11) but the resultant interactions with people and communities in public places became an important aspect of the Dancers' Workshop social and artistic practice. From the late 1960s onwards the Dancers' Workshop became directly involved in creating performances and events for and with specific communities engaging with the social and personal issues which were central to their lives.

Performance for Halprin has always been the outcome of process but the focus and intention of the processes she has used have transformed over the years resulting in a transformation of the style and structure of her performances. In the 1980s, moving away from theatrical performance, Halprin became increasingly involved in the creation of large-scale community myths and rituals, the enactment of personal or collective stories intended to create change in the lives of individuals and communities. This process, manifested in *Circle the Earth* and *The Planetary Dance*, is explored in depth in Chapter 3. Speaking with enthusiasm of the rituals of the Pomo Indians, Halprin refers to them as 'a mystical theatre. The people dance their prayers, their stories, their healings, and their dreams' (Halprin 1995: 245). In a contemporary western form, this is what Halprin's performance rituals have become.

Throughout her career Halprin has challenged the separation of audience and performer, eroding the distance between them by invading their physical space, undermining their emotional distance through both the form and content of her performances and ultimately inviting them to participate as co-creators or witnesses. There is no place for dispassionate observers in Halprin's work (Halprin 1995: 249). In her performance rituals, the audience are invited to abandon a position of non-engagement to become witnesses who enter into the intention of the ritual. Halprin gives them an active function to facilitate them participating in a meaningful way. The authenticity of their experience has become as important as the authenticity of the performers' expression.

THEATRICAL PERFORMANCES

Halprin's later years have seen an unexpected return to performing in conventional theatres. *Parades and Changes* (1965) and *Intensive Care* (2000), both performed at her *80th Year Retrospective* (2000), serve to illuminate the ground covered in the 40-year period between the early works of the San Francisco Dancers' Workshop and the theatrical performances of her maturity.

Parades and Changes

In the retrospective performance for the sake of historical accuracy, Halprin chose to reconstruct *Parades and Changes* as faithfully as possible working with young and attractive dancers and replicating the costumes of white shirts, dark trousers and lace up shoes. She acknowledges that the same score could have been performed by older people or women with breast cancer (Halprin 2001b) but this would clearly have created a dance with different layers of meaning and theatrical impact from the original. The sound score in the retrospective performance is a combination of the radio broadcast incorporating popular music used in the performances in the 1960s and a new live music score composed by San Francisco musicians Norman Rutherford and Peter Whitehead in the spirit of the original score.

The performance commences as the 11 dancers walk through the auditorium and line up on stage with their backs to the audience. Turning to face the audience they begin, each in their own time and in their own way, to slowly remove their clothes. Their faces are expressionless and the task is performed neutrally but they keep their eyes focused on the audience, never diverting their gaze to look at what they are doing. As they undress they fold their clothes neatly in front of them. The impact of the differently gendered bodies being revealed is disconcertingly strong even today; the uniformity of the clothes and the task emphasizing rather than minimizing the difference. Each dancer stands naked for a moment, vulnerable and ordinary before reversing the procedure, some dressing while others are still undressing. When they are dressed they begin to walk briskly in interweaving pathways around the stage accompanied by *Downtown*, a lively, popular 1960s song, in clear contrast to both the pace and quality of the movement in the ritual undressing. Returning to stillness scattered around the stage the dancers begin to undress again. This time their eyes are focused on another member of the company but since their gaze is not mutual they are unaware of who may be looking at them and from which direction. A web of gazes is cast across the space. The unwavering focus of the eyes is one of the most powerful elements in the dance. It magnifies the act of looking and being looked at which is crucial to all live performance, while also suggesting its centrality in our daily life encounters. It is unnerving in its intensity and its simplicity. The focus of their eyes means that the dancers are relying solely on touch to perform the undressing and dressing which heightens their, and the audience's, awareness of both the detail and the physicality of their gestures. In this repetition of the task the dancers not only inhabit the stage space more fully but their movements are also more expansive. Once again each dancer stands naked for a moment before dressing, then walks through the space in the same matter-of-fact manner as before. This time they stop close to and facing another member of the group, some in single sex pairs, others with a partner of the opposite sex. These pairs were not predetermined. The ritual continues, this time with an aura of intimacy and a heightened intensity as the partners gaze at one another. The actions continue to be performed with neutrality, the dancers' bodies moving closer and further from one another as necessitated by the task while their eyes remain in contact. Nothing else happens, there is no touch, no further exchange.

Once naked the dancers move towards long sheets of paper that have been unrolled across the stage. With the same singularity of purpose that they have applied to their previous actions they begin to tear the paper. Working as a group but without direct interaction, their whole bodies are engaged in the activity: stretching, reaching, twisting, rising or moving closer to the ground as the task demands. Orange or blue lights play across the bodies and the paper. The sound of the paper being torn becomes the soundtrack as the live music fades. The pace quickens as the pieces of paper become smaller and the dancers move with them cascading through the air. The beauty of this moving sound sculpture is undeniable; the nudity has become simply an aesthetic element of the work. One critic described it as 'a warm, pulsating, human sculpture' (Ulrich 2000).

Finally the dancers gather up all the scraps of paper to the accompaniment of another popular 1960s song. Walking to the front of the stage they stand with their arms heaped with paper concealing their nudity. Then, turning to leave, they reveal their naked behinds in a final image which is both mundane and ironically humorous.

The retrospective programme states that: 'this piece was created in reverence of the human form, as an extension of Halprin's work in the natural environment' (Dancers' Group Studio Theater 2000). Halprin professes an innocence when creating the original work claiming that it was a natural development from working in the sun on the dance deck in the 1960s when 'everyone took their clothes off to express community love and to shed capitalist trappings' (Howard 2000a). There is an anti-establishment agenda inherent in the work even if it was created with an element of naivety. Halprin describes it as 'breaking all the rules of corporate America' (Halprin 2001b). The idea for the 'Undressing and Dressing Dance' originated in a Gestalt workshop with Fritz Perls when Halprin reacted impulsively to a businessman, who for her represented conservative values, by aggressively and provocatively stripping in front of him (Halprin 1995: 111–12). While Halprin worked consciously to release these feelings of aggression in creating the score for *Parades and Changes* in favour of 'a more natural openness' (there is certainly no trace of aggression in the retrospective performance) the

Figure 2.2 *Parades and Changes*, 1996 retrospective. Photograph by Coni Beeson

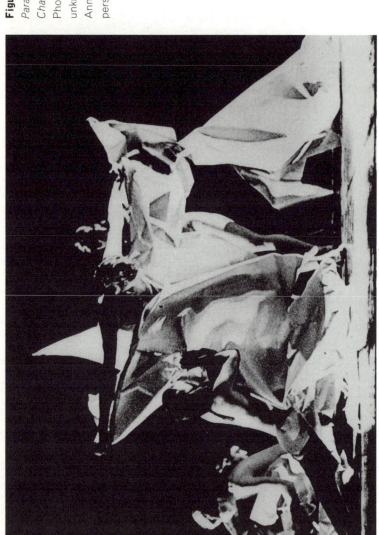

underlying challenge to corporate values remains. It is surely no coinci-
dence that the chosen costumes to some extent mirror the businessman's own.

Intensive Care

While providing a clear contrast in style *Intensive Care* reflects the values
and experience of the later period of Halprin's life and work as closely
as *Parades and Changes* does her early work. *Intensive Care* attempts to
confront the taboos surrounding death without illusion. The relationship of the content to Halprin's life experiences has already been
mentioned in Chapter 1. Although created as a piece of theatre for
Halprin, the structure of the performance intuitively reflected the Five
Stages of Healing (discussed in Chapter 3). The theme held a strong
personal resonance for two of the other performers apart from Halprin.
It had a particular urgency for Jeff Rehg who had danced in *Circle the
Earth, Dancing with Life on the Line* (1989 and 1991) and gave him an
opportunity for catharsis and personal healing. Suffering from both
AIDS and sarcoma cancer the process of creating the performance
enabled Rehg to accept and express his 'personal darkness' providing
the means to make it visible and to transform it (Rehg 2001: 56). The
performance also constituted a personal triumph for him as in 1997
he had been given only three to six months to live. Actor David
Greenaway, also in *Memories from My Closet*, drew on his experiences as
a care worker in a hospice. Lakshmi Aysola, the youngest dancer, represented the reality that death can strike at any age. Lakshmi, who also
performed in *Parades and Changes*, is trained in Butoh.

While the authenticity of the performances is crucial to fulfill
Halprin's purpose, aesthetic considerations played a central role in the
final presentation of the material. The minimal set reflects the stark-
ness of the theme, while the lighting design effectively signals and
supports the mood changes throughout the piece. *Intensive Care* begins
with the performers completely shrouded in cloths. They are isolated
from one another in a row at the back of the stage. This section emphasizes the loneliness of the individual in the face of death; it is raw and
highly charged. The performers emerge slowly from beneath the cloths,
their faces and bodies contorted by suffering, horror and distress. They
fall from the draped chairs to which they are confined, revealing the
vulnerability of their naked bodies beneath costumes modelled on

Figure 2.4 *Intensive Care*, 2000. Photograph by Coni Beeson

hospital gowns. Halprin's mouth is covered by a surgical mask, her head wrapped in a winding sheet. The performers' movements reflect a sense of despair and helplessness: trembling, rocking, hugging the cloth close to the body, hands clawing in the air, at their face, throat and hair, limbs loose and ineffectual, mouth moving half open or distorted in a silent scream. The electronic music composed and performed live by Miguel Frasconi is discordant, a sound evoking a heartbeat threaded through it. The score becomes increasingly grating, a protracted scream-like tone underpinning it. As it rises to a crescendo, the previously silent performers begin to shout. The dance becomes frenzied, Halprin and Greenaway throwing themselves around in their chairs, cloths flying, while Rehg remains motionless in a foetal position. Finally, as the music subsides into the sound of crying, the performers retreat into themselves curled on their chairs.

The mood of the next phase of the dance is calmer, the lighting softening to warm tones as the performers tentatively reach out to one another, their wheeled chairs silently gliding through the space. There is a period of respite and a tender exchange of touch, of warmth, of support and compassion as each individual makes contact with each of the others until the four of them come together. The audience is drawn in as a chorus of participants scattered among them whispers the words of terminally ill patients and the performers: 'Hold my hand', 'I'm so frightened', 'Don't leave me', 'I want to hold a baby'. But the reprieve is short lived and the group begins to be pulled apart as the enforced separation of death encroaches upon them. In desperation they clutch at one another but their chairs seem to move of their own accord spinning them away from one another until they are splayed against the back wall. The mournful tone of a shofar, a ram's horn trumpet, played on Yom Kippur (the Jewish Day of Atonement) is heard. The moment has come, an impersonal male voice tells them that 'It's time', asking 'Are you ready now?'; other phrases express love, fear and regret. The performers' movements become staccato, sometimes falling, casting huge shadows. Halprin unwinds the cloth around her head. Slowly leaving their chairs the performers begin to move forward accompanied by the haunting voice of Carol Swann singing live. There are moments of stillness. The lights dim tingeing the costumes with a bluish hue until only the figures are lit, becoming more like sculptural forms than bodies, as they gradually disappear beneath the stiff folds of the gowns and sink towards the floor. There is the sound of whispering, of breath. For Halprin this ending represents a return to natural forms, to rock and wind. It is a moving ending after the intensity of the performance, and the curtain call after it jars somewhat.

While striving to express the universality of the theme, Halprin acknowledges that *Intensive Care* has a particularly powerful impact for people facing death or caring for the dying. An intimate studio performance to an audience of doctors and nurses unleashed the buried feelings that it is not possible for them to express in the course of their work (Halprin 2001b). Halprin values the opportunity provided by such studio performances to process the audience's personal reactions through sharing and discussion. She continues to explore healing rituals that enable people to express their relationship to death. Together with Jeff Rehg she developed *Walking with the Dead*, a ritual created at Sea Ranch in response to the number of people in the Bay area who had lost friends to AIDS. Originally intended to be performed on All Hallows (1 November), the participants create a rich mandala in the natural environment and while walking its pathways, talk with loved ones they have lost before releasing their spirits. This ritual was performed in 2001 at Rehg's request after his death.

It is interesting to note that none of the performances in the retrospective significantly challenge the conventional use of theatrical space or the role of the audience, despite the whispering of the chorus among the audience in *Intensive Care*. This is perhaps because the nature of theatrical performance is no longer Halprin's primary concern. However, the radical features of her collaborative working processes, the transformation of authentic personal material into performance through the Life/Art Process and her use of 'direct movement' are clearly in evidence in *Intensive Care*. Both *Intensive Care* and *Parades and Changes* are being recreated for the Paris Festival d'Automne in 2004.

PERFORMANCE OR THERAPY?

Criticisms of her work as therapy rather than performance make no sense to Halprin quite simply because they imply that personal, emotional material is not appropriate for performance. It was precisely this split and the ensuing waste of 'the most powerful material that any artist could choose to work with' (Wolf 2000: 26) that Halprin began to challenge in the early years of the Dancers' Workshop:

> The person who is the performer is working with his body as an instrument
> . . . he's doing everything as if he were an object, when actually he's more than
> an object. He's full of the most fantastic psychological phenomena, but he's
> completely cutting these off and blocking them. These are the most unique
> parts of the performer . . . the dancer and the actor are their own instruments.
> They can find out why they are different from chairs or flutes or tape-recorders.
> (Halprin 1995: 97)

Halprin did not initially set out to provoke emotional material and was disconcerted when it began to emerge. She freely admits to being out of her depth in the early years but quickly recognized that, given the working processes she was engaged in, she needed to find ways to transform emotion artistically.

Although she is mindful of the well-being of participants when creating a performance or in a training workshop, Halprin demands that people work with their emotional material with as much attention, application, honesty and courage, as they bring to their physical work or other artistic content. She has little patience with malingerers but expects participants to actively engage with any emotional material which may be aroused by the working process. They must recognize that it is neither an irrelevant diversion nor an obstacle but a crucial component of their artistic resources, and use the processes that she offers to channel it creatively.

OTHER PRACTITIONERS

The qualities that Halprin admires in the work of other practitioners give a clear indication of her criteria for evaluating performance. In an interview with Richard Schechner in 1989 (Halprin 1995: 245–53) Halprin comments on a range of performances which have interested her, including the work of choreographer Martha Clarke (1944–), the Polish company Gardzienice, Robert Wilson (1941–), Liz Lehrman and Suzanne Lacy (1945–) (in addition to Peter Brook, Jerzy Grotowski, Eugenio Barba (1936–) and Eiko and Koma, see Chapter 1). The characteristics which attract her include 'raw power', emotional intensity, powerful physicality, sensuous beauty, the creative 'integration of voice, movment and imagery' and the ability of performers of either gender to embody both 'male and female' qualities. She respects performances which reflect or address social, political and cultural issues and the inclusiveness of the companies who use performers with physical limitations, older people or others with non-typical dance bodies. Halprin singles out Joseph Chaikin's monologue *The War in Heaven* (co-written with Sam Shepherd) performed after a debilitating stroke as particularly inspiring (Halprin 1995: 247–8). The relationship between the personal integrity required for such a performance and that in *Intensive Care* is clear.

MORE THAN THEATRE

It is inappropriate to focus attention on Halprin's theatrical performances, fascinating as they are, at the expense of her work in other environments or to highlight her earlier work with the San Francisco Dancers' Workshop over her later, less recognizably theatrical work. Major threads of her life's work have come to fruition in projects such as *Circle the Earth* and *The Planetary Dance*, which exemplify her work with communities and participatory ritual, and *Still Dance*, the powerful and evocative fruit of her years of work in the natural environment. Just as early in her career Halprin refused to be confined by artistic or social limitations her work continues to defy categorization, although she is aware of the temptation for critics or scholars to attempt to box her in (Halprin 1995: 247).

NATURE

Considering the importance of the natural environment in Halprin's work there is relatively little accessible written material that elucidates the approach and philosophy underlying this work. The experiential nature of her work and the personal and spiritual resonances it evokes mean that it is more difficult to articulate than other aspects of her work. Halprin's work in the environment sits uncomfortably within the confines of even a contemporary understanding of dance and perform-ance and yet it is a core aspect of her personal and artistic practice. Halprin claims that the 'sensual' landscape of California has 'become her theatre' (Anderson 1997) but how are we to understand this?

Since childhood Halprin has felt a deep sense of kinship with nature, experiencing the natural environment as a place of retreat, which offers her solace, nurturing, inspiration and wisdom. Her respect for, and sense of connection to, the environment has been informed by her experiences during her 30-year relationship with the Pomo Indians and her continuing interest in the culture of indigenous peoples. While she is adamant about the invalidity of attempting to appropriate indigenous beliefs or practices, she has been specifically attracted to the under-standing of the earth as 'a living entity' and to the healing power of nature (Halprin 1995: 214). Halprin believes that an increasingly urban and technological lifestyle has obscured our relationship to nature, reducing it to 'an inanimate object' which we attempt 'to exploit and control' (Halprin 1995: 214). Part of the intention of her work is to re-establish a sense of relatedness to the natural world:

> Clearly, there is a close and ancient rapport between humans and the natural environment. We have become too separate from this innate relationship, and we suffer a spiritual loss because of this . . . . I believe that reconnecting to nature will lend us a vocabulary for our art and for our lives . . . . It is my hope that this experiential contact with nature . . . will . . . move us . . . towards a deeper understanding of the sanctity of the earth and our place upon it.
>
> (Halprin 1995: 225)

Halprin's deep connection with nature has been shaped by her years of experience working on the dance deck, among the Redwood trees on her land, on the slopes of Mount Tamalpais above her home and at Sea Ranch. These environments have become imbued with decades of creative work and personal and collective explorations.

For Halprin the work in the environment generates a feeling of coming home, an 'inner satisfaction' coupled with a 'sense of liberation' which is in part due to an extended experience of time and space (Halprin 2001b). For her, the time frame changes with nature, 'everything slows down' and there is a sense of timelessness which allows one to flow with 'one's own internal rhythm' (2001b). The release from the compartmentalized experience of time and space in contemporary life is both restorative and invigorating. Halprin has also been influenced by the extended use of time in indigenous ritual.

In the 1960s Halprin fiercely resisted interpreting natural phenomena symbolically:

> When you are surrounded by movement in nature you look at the movement of a leaf or of light on a tree or a flock of birds. You are being saturated with movement in nature that doesn't have symbolism, nor characters. You soon identify yourself with these natural phenomena; you discover your body is a body . . . like a leaf is a leaf, a rock a rock. These things ARE; they do not stand for anything else.

> (Halprin c.1960s)

Creating dances on the dance deck in touch with the natural elements, Halprin experienced the apparently random nature of natural occurrences and sounds as 'a form of organisation . . . of continuity' (Halprin 2001b). Her perception of nature as interweaving different layers of experience in unpredictable ways became an inspiration in the construction of her early performance works. The sense of an underlying if arbitrary pattern is what distinguishes her approach at this time from Merce Cunningham's and John Cage's use of chance procedures in choreography and composition.

As Halprin's experiential relationship to nature has deepened its role in her work has also matured. Referring to natural forms such as rocks shaped by the ocean or tidal markings on the beach as 'perfect compositions . . . wonderful models for dances' she sees natural processes as 'a basic source for our aesthetic sensibilities' and poses the question 'How do we make dances reflecting the principles of nature?' (Halprin 1995: 216). Given the emphasis on process in her creative work, it is the processes of nature that interest Halprin providing inspiration for dance scores. She sees her work as 'reflective' rather than 'representational' of the natural world and does not attempt to represent its forms

Figure 2.5 *Seasons: Part One – Summer*, 2003. Photograph by Rick Chapman, San Francisco

either literally or symbolically. For Halprin, since we are part of nature, our bodies composed of the same elements as the earth and our lives shaped by the same cyclic patterns, it is possible 'to understand the natural world as a reflection of . . . human experience' (Halprin 1995: 216). The artistic inspiration that Halprin derives from nature is not primarily concerned with abstract aesthetics but is inherently connected to content and personal meaning. Halprin believes in an intrinsic connection between our inner world and the outer landscape. An embodied encounter with nature can become a metaphor for our life story offering us a new understanding of our human condition and potential healing of unresolved feelings or situations in our lives.

Despite this emphasis on personal meaning Halprin's starting point for environmental work is always physical. An 'experiential cycle' consisting of three phases (Contact, Explore, Respond) provides the basic structure for all her work in nature. After preparatory exercises to deepen sensory awareness and 'fine-tune our kinesthetic sense' (Halprin 1995: 218), for example a silent blindfold walk in the environment, the first phase of the cycle is introduced:

Contact: The whole body is used to physically connect with an element in the environment, for example a tree, rock or sand, absorbing its texture, weight, shape, movement, smell and sounds, becoming familiar with the materiality of the element through the physicality of the body and the senses. Working naked may facilitate this sensory exploration. Sufficient time must be allowed to ensure that participants have the opportunity to expand their awareness beyond their daily life perceptions. This stage is concerned with the here and now, what is actually present; it could involve making a realistic drawing of the element which is being worked with.

Explore: This second phase initiates a more active interaction with the element concerned. A full range of physical activities and tasks in relation to it are explored, for example, climbing, rolling, digging, sculpting, throwing. Responding physically to the variety of terrain and conditions in the environment challenges participants' habitual movement patterns extending their movement vocabulary and generating new creative resources.

Respond: This final phase entails a more subjective response as the feelings and personal associations with the element explored

surface. As these personal responses are expressed in movement and vocally in the environment meaning begins to
emerge. Drawing and writing may be used to bring the underlying meaning more clearly into consciousness.

The three phases of this process allow participants to experience a sense
of identification with an element in nature and to explore and express
their personal 'mythology' in relation to it. Frequently Halprin will suggest working with two contrasting elements, then exploring a synthesis
of the two. For Halprin, meaning evolves organically over time as a result
of the process which if rushed becomes superficial (Halprin 2001b). Her
experiences with the Pomo Indians have validated Halprin's intuitive
acceptance of an individual's personal experiences in nature however
mysterious they may seem. She believes that such experiences empower
people and has no difficulty in respecting that a tree may become 'a sacred
symbolic metaphor' for an individual because they have 'endowed it with
personal experience' (Halprin 2001b).

In 'Earth Dances' Halprin describes how using the Life/Art Process
in the natural environment enabled a participant in a workshop at Sea
Ranch to come to terms with his partner's death and offered him a way
to move forward in his life (Halprin 1995: 212–25). Rick Lepore's intuitive response to a movement task and an element in the environment,
dragging pieces of driftwood across the beach and arranging them on a
steep cliff face, became a ritual enactment of his experience of the final
stages of his partner's life. The symbolic meaning of the ritual was initially unconscious and only became clear through visualizations (Halprin
1995: 221). Halprin believes that such rituals are 'discovered' rather
than 'created' (Halprin 1995: 219) as a result of a kinaesthetic interaction with the environment which also engages our emotions and
personal associations. Through the encounters with the environment a
deep intuitive knowledge is awakened in the individual.

Halprin refers to 'spontaneous group rituals' which arise as a result
of the collective experience of working with this approach, claiming
that such rituals 'emerge as creations of the earth itself' (Halprin 1995:
222–5). This statement reflects Halprin's experience of the natural
world as a collaborator in her creative work. There is a strong sense of
relationship in Halprin's work in the environment, it becomes a partner
in her dance. Although specific associations will be evoked for her as a
result of working at a certain site Halprin feels that the essence of these

associations can subsequently be transferred elsewhere even to a theatre space (Butler and McHugh 2001: 49). She does not feel that it is possible to generalize about which themes will be evoked in specific environments. While acknowledging that certain elements or environments may elicit specific movement responses, Halprin points out that each element tends to offer us contrasting qualities: rock can be supportive or resistant, wind fierce or caressing (Halprin 2001b).

While Halprin recognizes that there are no absolute rules for working artistically in the natural environment, she prefers to avoid introducing extraneous sound/music or man-made materials which may distract from what is already there (Halprin 2001b). The use of the naked body is also part of this 'natural' aesthetic. Natural occurrences such as a flock of birds flying overhead or the sound of the ocean are seen as an intrinsic part of a performance (Halprin 2001b). Halprin imparts an aware and respectful attitude to nature to her students, encouraging them to be conscious of any changes they make in the environment and to dismantle anything they have created when they have finished.

STILL DANCE (1981–)

In 1981 Eeo Stubblefield created *Still Dance* with the dual intent of creating an 'internal, ephemeral experience for the performer' as well as a 'permanent visual piece, the photograph' (Stubblefield 2001). An exhibition of many of the *Still Dance* photographs with Halprin as the performer was shown at Halprin's *80th Year Retrospective* (2000) and other venues. This, combined with Andy Abrahams Wilson's award-winning film (Grand Jury Prize from the International On Camera Festival in 2003) of Stubblefield's and Halprin's collaborative process in making *Still Dance*, has brought greater public recognition of one aspect of Halprin's work in nature. The collaboration, initiated by Stubblefield, consisted of her photography, body art and site preparation with Halprin's dance exploration of each site. 'We come with our story, respond to the land's larger power, and a new story emerges' (Stubblefield 2001).

Each photograph shows Halprin in the land, her body covered in such materials as paint, mud, wood rot, thin white cloth or bundles of straw. Stubblefield describes the choice of colour and texture of the materials she uses as emerging from her response to a particular site 'from the interplay of both the character of the story and direct observation of the land' (2001). These elicited differing responses from

Figure 2.6 *Still Dance*, 'Anna Halprin Log Series', 1999. Photograph © Eeo Stubblefield

Halprin, but her trust in Stubblefield's 'strong visual sense' encouraged her to explore even those coverings that seemed most alien to her (Halprin 2001b). Though accustomed to moving naked in nature, Halprin is clear that for this project she welcomed Stubblefield's body painting as both an aesthetic response to each place and as a means of preventing the work becoming 'too personal and literal' (Halprin 2001b). Sites were selected near Sea Ranch and around Stubblefield's home in the Catskills, in New York State. The working process varied according to time available and the demands of the site. Stubblefield notes that

> Halprin's willingness and ability to transcend the initial [experience] of some of the harsh conditions, such as freezing water, uninviting mud flats, and middle of the night cliff adventures was truly inspiring and reinforced their shared bond of working in the environment.

> (2004b)

The body art alters the way that the performer is seen in relation to the natural surrounds, for instance it can emphasize the blend of body and land or reveal a stark contrast between them. In 'Log Series', Halprin's naked body, covered in tree rot, seems to merge with the hollowed out tree in which she lies. She is only just distinguishable from the tree, like a relief image in stone. While in 'Underworld Series' she sits by a muddy pool beneath a dense mass of ferns with trees towering above in a green brown subterranean world yet her body is painted bright blue. The choice of colour initially shocked Halprin but 'knowing Eeo has a keen eye' (Halprin 1997–2000) she went ahead and recognized that indeed 'the blue brought the sky into the site and the contrast of the vivid blue against the earthly tones was beautiful . . .' (Halprin 1997–2000). As she 'began to adorn' herself with the mud around her until her body blended with the cave (Halprin 1997–2000), she experienced 'a feeling of reverence' combined with a sense of 'accepting the body of an ageing woman' (Halprin 2001b). On entering the cave she had a sense of both being buried and being in the womb. In these two examples, as in other of the photographs, Halprin and Stubblefield appear to be confronting and working creatively with the processes of ageing, death and dying. Rather than being a lugubrious task, the images reveal an unflinching view of the gamut of emotions expressed by Halprin in her explorations on each site. Many photographs, like the performer merged with the tree, suggest death and earth's ultimate absorption of the disintegrating body, but others show Halprin's acceptance, respect and pleasure in her 80-year-old body and the continued joy and exhilaration of working with natural elements and forces. This aspect of the project is considered in more detail in Andy Abrahams Wilson's film *Returning Home* (2003).

RETURNING HOME

The 45-minute film balances a documentary style, showing preparations for the dances with particular focus on the application of the various body coverings, with extended shots of the dances themselves. The sparse but evocative music of Fred Frith enhances the connection between the documentary and performance aspects of the film. At times Halprin, disgruntled, expresses fear at the danger that the wood or soil being applied to her body will get into her eyes, or bemused disbelief that she tolerates such a cold, dark and uncomfortable journey to an unknown site. However, the process of physical transformation acts as a crucial period of preparation for performance: 'This body art helps to prepare the performer to move out of the ordinary realm, as well as to attempt to give the viewer the chance to go with them' (Stubblefield 2004a). Once working in the site Halprin shows no sign of discomfort as she responds to the stimuli around and from within. Startling juxtapositions abound such as a sequence with Halprin working amidst fires on a beach at night which conjured up the image that she was dead. In her candid notes on the dances she recalls: 'Lying in the center of the surrounding fire lights on the sandy beach reminded me of Frida Kahlo's painting of her death burial' (Halprin 1997–2000). This is followed by a sequence of her walking through the burnt out remains of her house at Sea Ranch that tragically caught fire the following year after the *Still Dance* mentioned above. Perhaps the most surprising of the dances shown on the film is the final one in which an elegiac mood is abandoned in favour of a comic clowning sequence. Life and art merge seamlessly for a moment as Halprin's patience runs out during the completion of a body covering of bundles of straw. As the sun goes down and in an act of impatience Halprin rebels and storms off down the uneven path in search of a distant patch of warm sun. Despite Stubblefield calling her back to remove her shoes, Halprin continues to stomp on, turning sporadically to shake fists of straw defiantly at those left behind. In the rhythm of the repetitions and slight exaggerations of the lurching gait as she adjusts to the uneven path and her ungainly straw body, there is a sense of the consummate performer able to observe and exploit personal reaction to create full-bodied performance. The comic element with a poignant edge is a reminder of Halprin's early days as a comedienne on the New York stage and it reveals the 'freedom of imagination' and 'child-like nature' that Stubblefield notes as her original reason for being drawn to work with Halprin (*Returning Home* 2003).

3

THE MOUNTAIN
PERFORMANCES,
CIRCLE THE EARTH AND
THE PLANETARY DANCE

BACKGROUND AND EVOLUTION

In 1981 Halprin embarked on a project which would sow the seeds for a major strand of her work for the next 20 years, work which is still evolving in the early years of the twenty-first century. Initiated with her husband Lawrence, as a local community project, entitled 'A Search for Living Myths and Rituals through Dance and the Environment', it unexpectedly evolved into a five-year cycle of performances and community events inspired by Mount Tamalpais, where the Halprins live and work. In 1985 this transformed into *Circle the Earth*, a large-scale ritual performance which was recreated and performed in several countries until 1991. *The Planetary Dance*, a global participatory dance ritual, grew out of *Circle the Earth* and developed alongside it from 1987 onwards. *The Planetary Dance* continues to be performed, in spring each year, by communities and groups across the globe.

Through this ongoing process Halprin has developed her practice and thinking concerning performance and ritual and working with communities. In the course of its evolution she has explored the relevance of myth and ritual in the contemporary world, pushing the boundaries of dance as a transforming medium for individuals and communities, a means of healing on a personal, community and global scale, and an effective tool for social action. Halprin refers to it as a dance which 'has been many years in the making, as many years as I have lived. It is the largest manifestation of my own search for a dance of meaning, content and spirit' (Halprin with Kaplan 1995: 1).

THE MOUNTAIN PERFORMANCES

'A Search for Living Myths and Rituals' began as a series of workshops with members of the Halprins' local community in Marin, California. The series was envisaged as 'a search for a myth with a community vision', an opportunity for the Halprins to explore 'the mythology of the collective' (Halprin with Kaplan 1995: 8) using collective creativity. For Anna Halprin it marked a broadening of her work with students at the San Francisco Dancers' Workshop and the Tamalpa Institute in personal and creative process, to a community-orientated approach. Lawrence Halprin's contribution was crucial since he had been 'working with groups of people around issues of community development in relationship to the environment' (Halprin with Kaplan 1995: 8). The project and its subsequent developments also signalled a return for Anna Halprin to public performance. The mountain performances were performed by Tamalpa dancers in a local theatre and were followed by a community event. *Circle the Earth* involved a minimum of 100 performers and an audience of witnesses. With *The Planetary Dance* the performance element, together with any notion of audience, dropped away as the event became a participatory ritual.

In the 'Living Myths and Rituals' workshops the Halprins used art, movement and the environment to draw the community participants together, creating a context and shared language to facilitate the emergence of a group myth. They had no preconceived idea about what would evolve. Early in the workshops the image of a mountain kept recurring; more than an archetypal image this theme had poignant local significance. The community was located at the base of Mount Tamalpais, a beautiful natural reserve usually widely enjoyed by the public, steeped in legend and seen by Anna Halprin as 'the spiritual center of our area' (Halprin with Kaplan 1995: 8). At that time the trails on the mountain had been closed because several women had been murdered by a serial killer who was still at large. Through the workshops the mountain emerged as a 'living myth' central to the community, with a clear connection to the participants' lives. 'We discovered our need to reclaim the mountain in order to reclaim our sense of community and vision' (Halprin with Kaplan 1995: 9). The project culminated in

In the Mountain, On the Mountain, a two-day event created in response to this need. *In the Mountain* was a ritual theatre performance by dancers from the Tamalpa Institute (including Halprin) with a chorus of participants from the 'Living Myths and Rituals' project. The performance ritual was divided into three parts, Initiation, Offerings and Regeneration, imagined to be taking place in the heart of the mountain. It was dedicated to the spirit of the mountain, the Miwaks, the indigenous people who lived beneath her including those among them who had lost their lives, and the women who were killed on the trails. The purpose of the performance is clearly stated:

> It is our intention to evoke the spirit of the mountain through our performance and to feel a unified sense of community . . . . We hope this performance will inspire you to become your own performers, and to find your own personal and collective myths tomorrow 'On the Mountain' as we do a ritualized walk down its trails. The walk will symbolize the re-investment of hope and the rebirth of Spring.
>
> (Tamalpa Institute 1981)

This was a performance in which the life of a community in crisis was clearly interwoven. Community participation had furnished the central theme of the performance, which included ritual re-enactments of the violence. Friends and relations of the victims were in the audience. There was tension as people wondered if the murderer might attend the performance.

During the night of the performance in *Passage*, a preparation for the community ritual the next day, participants were encouraged to create their own rituals and ceremonies culminating in a sunrise ceremony. On the second day, *On the Mountain*, 80 members of the community of all ages, invited to wear white, travelled up the mountain by bus. As a group they walked to the summit to view the four directions which had been invoked in the performance. Participants were asked to consider what they wanted to restore in their lives. There was a silent ritualized walk down the trails; offerings, including poetry, meditations, music, song and a tree planting, were made at the sites of the murders 'as a way of marking these tragedies, and affirming the community's need to reclaim the mountain' (Halprin with Kaplan 1995: 9). The procession was completed carrying bamboo poles and a panel from the *Running Fence* by the well-known artist Christo, objects that had been invested with symbolic significance during the performance, and culminated in a sunset ceremony.

Two days later the police were alerted by an anonymous telephone call. Three weeks later the killer, who had been active for two years, was captured. While not claiming direct causality between the ritual and the killer's arrest, Halprin is clear that the two events are related: 'In one sense we performed a prayer and our prayer was answered' (Halprin 1995: 230). What is clear is that a ritual had been created and enacted, which effectively reclaimed a site of significance to local people, a site that had been desecrated by violence and had become unsafe for them. The Halprins' search for an authentic living myth and ritual empowered a community paralysed by fear, by a combination of expression and action through an interaction of the arts and the environment. The outcome was more far reaching than the Halprins had anticipated.

The next year (1982) a dance of thanksgiving was created to commemorate the end of the murders and the renewal of the mountain. Perhaps this would have been the end of the sequence if it had not been for Don Jose Mitsuwa, an indigenous Huichol shaman who came to the Tamalpa Institute to present a deer dance ceremony. He commended what had taken place on the mountain, describing it as 'one of the most sacred places on earth' (Halprin with Kaplan 1995: 9) but commented that it would be necessary to dance there for five years in order for the purification to be successful. Halprin followed this advice and created mountain dances for the following three years. The synchronicity that marked the first event continued, as it took five years to convict the murderer.

While the essential theme of the dances remained the struggle of life against death, each year the performances had a different emphasis. *Return to the Mountain* (1983) was the first one to be described as a peace dance. It included a dance inspired by animal imagery and a ceremony for peace between people and the environment. Don Jose was invited to participate in the ceremony on the summit of the mountain. *Run to the Mountain* (1984) was a dance for peace among all the peoples of the world. Running was the central motif 'because running is common to all people and helps communicate the urgency for peace within ourselves, with each other, with our communities, our nations and throughout the world' (Tamalpa Institute 1984). In the lead up to the performance the company of Tamalpa Dancers ran with brightly coloured banners across Golden Gate Bridge. The audience were gradually becoming more involved in the performance, participating in communal running dances. At the beginning of the mountain ceremony on the day after, the performance runners, including members of the audience, ran up the mountain from the four directions. The spiritual leaders invited to participate alongside Don Jose now included a representative from the American Indian Council of Marin and a Presbyterian minster.

Circle the Mountain, a Dance in the Spirit of Peace (1985) completed the five-year cycle and marked a radical change in structure that prefigured its transformation into *Circle the Earth*. The dance embodied a vision of world peace, 'the underlying objective is to make a vivid statement for mutual understanding and peace – one that can be taken from its performance here and shared with many people in many places' (Tamalpa Institute 1985).

Halprin felt that a small performance company was no longer a potent enough vehicle for such a vision. She aimed to create a dance with 100 participants, so that the scale of the vision would be matched by the scale of the performance:

> Making a peace dance, like making peace is not a small task. It takes the harmony of many to stop a war that only a few might begin. So our peace dance needs the commitment of more than two, or ten, or twenty, or even fifty performers. I am seeking 100 performers. One hundred performers to create a circle large enough for clear images of peace to come through. One hundred performers to create a spirit voice, strong enough so that our peaceful song is heard and our peaceful steps felt.

> The weapons of war have a critical mass. So too do the hopes of peace. We need 100 performers, 200 feet, to dance upon the planet for its life and its healing – to find a dance that inspires us to keep the earth alive.

> (Tamalpa Institute 1985)

Halprin offered a nine-day workshop to prepare the participants who were no longer all Tamalpa trained. The second day (Easter Sunday, Buddha's birthday and the day after Passover) was spent in a ritual celebration on the mountain. Lawrence Halprin was actively involved in the group's preparation for the mountain celebration, as he had been in 'Living Myths and Rituals'. Bill Wahpehpeh from the Kickapoo and Sac and Fox tribe in Oklahoma, head of the international Indian Treaty Council, participated in the ceremony on the mountain, continuing the

involvement of Native Americans. During the workshop Halprin collaborated with composer Terry Riley who created a new composition for
voices for the performance. On the eighth day *Circle the Mountain* was
performed to an audience of invited witnesses. The intention had broadened from restoring peace on the mountain to peace on the planet. The
dance renamed itself *Circle the Earth* and began to travel. In 1985 it was
recreated in sites across America including the United Nations Plaza
and Central Park, New York.

CIRCLE THE EARTH

A contemporary peace dance ritual for 100 performers, *Circle the Earth*
was recreated in Marin, California, at Easter in 1986, 1987 and 1988.
The format continued to be a nine-day workshop, with the second day
spent in ceremonies on Mount Tamalpais, culminating in the performance. By 1987 the scores which formed the basic structure of *Circle the
Earth* were clearly articulated although they continued to evolve. Many
of the scores developed elements from the earlier mountain performances including running, honouring the four directions and the theme
of restoration. Each year had a different emphasis. In 1987 participants
were given the choice of working with Halprin or with vocalist Susan
Osborn on a new musical score. In 1988, inspired partly by the events
in Chernobyl, the whole event was held on the Marin headlands and
the focus was on our connection with the natural environment. Every
year the story of the original dance on the mountain and the capture of
the killer was reiterated. This repetition served to re-enforce the event
as a contemporary myth. From 1986 onwards *Circle the Earth* travelled
not only across America, including being performed at the American
Dance Festival and Esalen, but to Europe including Germany (Freiburg
and Essen), Switzerland (outside Zurich 1989), Italy (Mont Blanc) and
to Australia (Melbourne 1987) and Bali. Its growth was unprecedented.
In 1987, in order to respond to the interest worldwide and to allow
communities in different countries to participate in their own way,
Halprin created *The Planetary Dance*, based on the 'Earth Run' score in
Circle the Earth, which is still being performed in 2003.

   Circle the Earth continued to be performed and in 1989 there was
another major shift in emphasis. *Circle the Earth*, *Dancing with Life on the
Line* confronted AIDS, a crisis which was threatening the community

Figure 3.1
Circle the Earth at Kirby Cove, 1988. Photograph by Jay Graham

around San Francisco and in which Halprin had become involved through her work in the healing arts. 'From the killer on the mountain, to the killer in the world, we now journey inside to confront the potential killer within ourselves' (Tamalpa Institute 1989). Participants included members of two groups Halprin had been working with: STEPS Theatre Company for People Challenging AIDS and Women with Wings for Women Challenging AIDS through Dance and Ritual. AIDS was still seen as a frightening taboo surrounded by ignorance and prejudice. Halprin confronted this taboo head-on:

> Among the dancers this year will be men and women in various states of wellness after exposure to the HIV virus. Their healing journey will be the focus of the 1989 performance of *Circle the Earth*. But *Circle the Earth* is not just for people who are HIV+; it is for all of us. We need to dance together.

> AIDS is a crisis of the body, and in this crisis it is important the body speak in its own language – movement. AIDS touches not only those who face it, but also those who do not. This year we ask <u>YOU</u> to dance with those among us who are fighting for life, to support the commitment and honor the courage of our brothers and sisters who are challenging AIDS.

> (Tamalpa Institute 1989)

This version of *Circle the Earth* was the culmination of the work of all the previous years. For Halprin it was 'the first time where our goal was not at a distance from the ritual itself' (Tamalpa Institute 1989). The personal and collective crises addressed were totally interconnected. Like the first performance of *In the Mountain, On the Mountain, Dancing with Life on the Line* was addressing an immediate and specific issue. The intensity of both the process and the performance reflected the immediacy of the crisis for all concerned, participants and witnesses alike. It closely paralleled Halprin's own experiences dealing with cancer and she led the participants with passion in the performance. In this performance her long-term concern with healing was fully integrated in the artistic process. The effects of *Dancing with Life on the Line* were so far reaching that this version of *Circle the Earth* was recreated in 1991. This was the last time that *Circle the Earth* was performed in its entirety, although Halprin continued to work with elements of it in *The Planetary Dance* and in workshops.

THE PLANETARY DANCE

With the increase of requests for *Circle the Earth* to be run in different parts of America and the world, it became clear that Halprin would not be able to facilitate them all. Although other facilitators had been trained by Halprin to run *Circle the Earth*, if the dance was to grow into a global form as she had envisaged, '100 communities world-wide performing this dance simultaneously via satellite' (Tamalpa Institute 1986b), it would be necessary to create a simpler form. The new dance ritual, called *The Planetary Dance*, was based on the 'Earth Run' section from *Circle the Earth* since this was a dance that 'would be accessible to many people, no matter where they lived' (Halprin with Kaplan 1995: 11). The flyer that went out to friends, colleagues and former students in 1987 explained that the intention was to create a worldwide perform-ance in the spirit of peace with all those who had touched *Circle the Earth*.

It was never Halprin's intention that the Marin format for the dance should be slavishly adhered to across the world and one reason for select-ing the 'Earth Run' from *Circle the Earth* was that, as a closed score, it was the easiest to facilitate and follow. As a ritual it was self-contained. More significantly the activity itself acted as a metaphor for the intention of achieving 'harmony and peace in our lives' through its demand for group awareness 'as people run together – accommodating each others' phys-ical capabilities and speeds' in a 'moving act of Peace' (Planetary Dance Board 1988). Although the instructions for the score were precise, offering a unity of purpose and activity, there was emphasis in the invi-tation to participating groups on two ways that the dance could be made to resonate with the local community's needs/character as well as the global intention. Groups were invited to 'frame the score (preparation and closure) in different ways – a ceremony, ritual, blessing, or dance pertaining to something special in your community or culture . . .' (Halprin 1987) or to change some of the resources in the 'Earth Run' score, particularly the spoken text. If, even with these suggestions, it was not possible to organize a run, then there were other ways that individ-uals or families could participate through, for instance, doing the 'Peace Dance Meditation' (part of the first preparatory score for *Circle the Earth*).

While from 1987 to 1991 *The Planetary Dance* in Marin ran along-side *Circle the Earth*, from 1992 onwards it settled into a regular day-long format that varied slightly each year in response to the chosen issue and altering community involvement. Each spring the event began with a group of all ages greeting the sunrise with ceremonies and songs, many having run to the summit of Mount Tamalpais. The men's and women's rituals that took place simultaneously on local beaches became regular features of the day. All groups met at a site on the mountain to share readings, stories and interdenominational prayers before rehearsing for the 'Earth Run'. At this point greetings from other groups taking part in the dance from many parts of the world were read out, reaffirming the global nature of the dance ritual. Halprin then led everyone in a long snake into a carefully prepared site to form a square of kneeling people within a circle (defined by flour and banked straw in *The Planetary Dance* 2002). With drummers and musicians playing to keep a regular pulse and help the runners maintain energy and focus the 'Earth Run' was performed in a series of concentric circles.

While extra runs might be included for the children or 'in memory of loved ones who have died' (Halprin and friends 1995), the essence of the dance remained the same. This included each dancer voicing a dedication for their run, and a unified intention to dance '[a] prayer for peace among people and peace with the Earth' (Halprin and Planetary Dance Community 2002). The day concluded with thanksgiving, music and a feast.

Since this was a global dance ritual, it was important to set up lines of communication that would allow groups to grasp the size and impact of the whole event. Halprin had requested feedback from all those who had participated in the first *Planetary Dance* (1987) and due to time differences across the world this began to arrive by phone, first from Amanda Levy in New Zealand before the dance had even begun in Marin. Over the next few months Halprin 'received word from groups in Switzerland, Australia, Germany, Spain, Mexico, Israel, England, Egypt, New Zealand, Indonesia, India and many places in the United States' (Halprin 1987). By 1996, as Halprin had envisaged, *The Planetary Dance* had been performed by over 2000 people in 37 countries. The dance continues to be performed each spring across the world but by 2002 Halprin no longer knew how many people from how many countries take part as it had become too large to track.

THE 'LIVING MYTH'

Despite the radical changes that took place during the creation of the mountain dances, *Circle the Earth* and *The Planetary Dance*, there are continuous threads that link them, as emphasized by the recent publicity that states 2002 will be the '22nd annual world-wide Planetary Dance' (Halprin and Planetary Dance Community 2002). Although there have not been 22 years of *The Planetary Dance*, the connections between the different forms are seen to be sufficiently strong and significant to be acknowledged in this way. Some of the major contributory elements that have supported the longevity and expansion of the dance, from its early performance structure through to its current participatory form, are considered below.

In 1987 Halprin described the score for *The Planetary Dance* as 'open-ended and self-renewing', adding that: 'It could be the recycling score to all future *Planetary Dances*' (Planetary Dance Board 1988). Judging by the version held on Mount Tamalpais (2002) and in many locations around the world, this has remained the case. The essential 'ingredients' pinpointed in 1988 were all apparent, yet it was not a tired repetition of the same material, but an invigorating, heartfelt, community response to new challenges that had arisen through the year. In the wake of the attacks on America on 11 September 2001, the escalation of violence between Israelis and Palestinians and the fear of nuclear war between India and Pakistan, tension was evident amongst the participants of the spring 2002 *Planetary Dance*. Although much of the structure remained the same, changes were made in the choice of text and in the way the four directions were marked in the walk around the peak of Mount Tamalpais. These reflected a sense of urgency in the need to look beyond America to forge greater links and understandings across nations. Individual dedications for the 'Earth Run' were highly charged as news arrived of the dance rituals being held in New York's Central Park and in different countries around the world. Making room for the individual statement of commitment to act for 'peace among people and peace with the earth' (Halprin and Planetary Dance Community 2002) was just one of the means by which *The Planetary Dance* shifted and stayed vibrant year after year.

From the original exploration that the Halprins undertook in their 1980–1 workshops 'A Search for Living Myths and Rituals through Dance and the Environment', the idea of the 'living myth' has remained crucial. It was described as:

> a narrative pattern giving significance to our existence, whether we invent or discover its meaning. A myth is not a fantasy or an untruth. It is a true story we discover in our bodies, and it is both unique and common to us all.
>
> (Halprin with Kaplan 1995: 4)

Figure 3.2 *The Planetary Dance*, dawn on Mount Tamalpais, 1993. Photograph by Jay Graham

Every year the original 'myth' of the killings on Mount Tamalpais was retold as a reminder of both the history of the event and the purpose of this particular style of dance ritual. While the retelling of the 'myth', along with other actions and ceremonies directly echoed previous dances, repetitions alone would not keep the dance alive. There were more fundamental issues facing contemporary society that needed to be addressed: 'We live in a society fractured by differences and a series of dishonored tribal and cultural affiliations. The absence of a solid community base creates a spiritual and social vacuum that needs to be filled' (Halprin with Kaplan 1995: 4).

From the start in 1981, it was clear that the performance must address the community's shared cause and desire for action. In shaping this first dance and the subsequent performance/rituals, Halprin used terms such as myth, ritual, ceremony and prayer in conjunction with dance and performance. This opened out the original community need to a broader perspective, suggesting that a higher power be engaged or contacted. The issue of spirituality and belief systems that this approach raised is a vexed one, since a premise of the work was to engage with a society fractured by differences who do not share religious beliefs or indeed see religion as relevant to their lives. How then is it possible to call upon a 'higher power'? Whose symbols and rituals are they?

Halprin refers to the centrality of the 'living myth' throughout the performance series because she values individual input bound by a common intention. In taking part in the dances it is necessary to recognize both the importance of creating a community with shared tasks reflective of a joint intention, combined with an acknowledgement of the differences each person brings from their own community. The individual's contribution and story is essential to the growth of the collective myth and is one of the reasons for Halprin's insistence that contemporary ritual making should not import wholesale, established rituals from a particular religion or culture. Halprin's close contact with Native Americans and particularly with the people of the Pomo Tribe, into which she was initiated, has had a profound and lasting influence on her beliefs. However, she is adamant that the way to find and develop 'living myths' is not through the appropriation of ancient or indigenous peoples' myths and rituals:

> The history of Western culture is largely one of the exploitation and destruction of indigenous cultures. We must return to the resources that are really our own – our bodies and our experiences – to forge a new way of honoring peace and human dignity.
>
> (Halprin with Kaplan 1995: 5)

From 1981 onwards the history of the performance has been enriched year by year through the 'gifts' of those who participated in it. This enabled the piece to renew itself in kaleidoscopic fashion as fragments gifted by a particular year, individual or group shifted into central focus and others moved to the periphery. For instance elements in the ceremonies that connect with Native American practices were present through Native American participation in the dance. In another country entirely other symbols and activities would emerge in response to the needs of the local community.

There is no doubt that the project the Halprins assigned themselves – the search for 'living myths' – was ambitious. It involved the community in answering some 'fundamental questions' about individual and group identity combined with how these might connect with the environment, 'attitudes about life and death' and what spiritual values the group embraced (Halprin 1995: 5). If the 'myth' in Halprin's termin-ology is uncovering the stories around those basic questions then the term 'ritual' refers to the enactment or performance of the myth through whole group participation.

Encapsulated in the idea of the 'living myth' is a sense of fluidity of content that can adapt to political, community or circumstantial changes. In her evaluation of the 1994 *Planetary Dance* Halprin notes the importance of finding a balance within the relationship between tradi-tion and experimentation in order to achieve this: 'In order to make rituals that create change, we need to remain in an experimental mode, while holding fast to the elements of our rituals that are weighted in time' (Halprin 1995: 236). This balance has been supported consistently through the contribution of many artists of different disciplines. Some have stayed involved over many years, while for others it has been a passing connection, but their role in collaborating on the projects has been essential to its growth and vitality. For example *The Planetary Dance* (2002) was coloured by contributions of giant painted puppets at the entrance to Santos Meadows, oral poetry, drumming, singing and vio-lin playing at the centre of the 'Earth Run' and, at its close, classical melodies by a virtuoso whistler. Many of those who contributed through their art form or in other ways have been engaged from the start of the mountain dances. While just as welcome have been newcomers, such as the teenage group from two local schools who had worked together to offer short songs or poems and to begin the 'Earth Run' (2002).

The variety and creativity of the dances performed around the world were shown in the photographs and documentation that arrived in Marin after each *Planetary Dance*. They testified to the success of another type of collaborative process that could operate across distance and over time. Halprin's vision for a global peace dance entailed those who had taken part in *The Planetary Dance* initiating new forms in their own coun-tries or communities. This would 'keep the material truly alive and creative' (Halprin 1987) in a process best illustrated through recount-ing her reaction to the growth of a sweet pea in her garden. While preparing for *The Planetary Dance* (2002) she spoke with pride of the sweet peas she had cultivated, but noted with a combination of curios-ity and pique that one single plant dwarfed the others with its rich blossom, stature and luxuriant growth. She had not planted this one, it had self-seeded in the best possible spot, watered by a drip from the tap, in semi-shade protected from harsh sun and wind. The innocuous

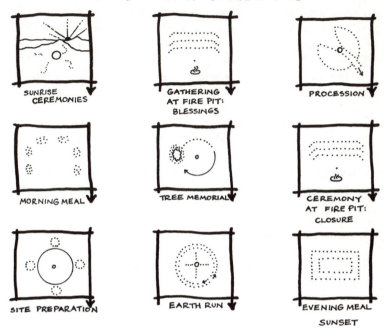

PLANETARY DANCE 1993

SUNRISE CEREMONIES

GATHERING AT FIRE PIT: BLESSINGS

PROCESSION

MORNING MEAL

TREE MEMORIAL

CEREMONY AT FIRE PIT: CLOSURE

SITE PREPARATION

EARTH RUN

EVENING MEAL SUNSET

Figure 3.3 Score for *The Planetary Dance*, artwork by Taira Restar, 2004, based on scores for the 1993 dance. A drawing on paper

comment on the resilient self-seeder became a running metaphor for the way that participants in *The Planetary Dance* could begin the dance in their own community, finding just the right conditions and context for it to thrive (Halprin 2002a).

THE RSVP CYCLES

The use of the RSVP Cycles has been an essential tool in the collective creative process of the mountain performances, *Circle the Earth* and *The Planetary Dance*. While the aspects summarized above have tended to support the continuity and growth of each dance over time and across distance, this has been made possible through the use of a form that, like a flexible skin, can both contain and respond to the shifting internal elements. As a framework the RSVP Cycles allow even large groups to retain clarity in what is potentially a chaotic process. This is achieved through making the creative process visible, allowing opportunities for the entire group to participate and using the cyclical nature of the RSVP model to emphasize process rather than goal. The definitions of each of the four elements that make up the RSVP Cycles have varied slightly over time and according to context. As applied to *Circle the Earth* they have been defined as follows:

R stands for Resources, which are the basic materials we have at our disposal. These include human and physical resources and their motivation and aims.

S stands for Scores, The word scores is derived from its original use in music which makes it possible to instruct groups of people to carry out prescribed activities. They delineate place, time, space and people, as well as sound and other related elements.

V stands for Valuaction, a coined term meaning 'the value of the action,' or the analysis, appreciation, feedback, value building and decision-making that accompanies the process of creation.

P stands for Performance, the implementation of the scores, which includes the particular style of the piece.

(Halprin with Kaplan 1995: 23)

The following section includes a detailed discussion of how each element contributes to the *Circle the Earth* workshop/performance process and how in any combination: 'Each part had its own internal significance, but got really cracking when it related to the others' (Halprin, L. 1969: 2). For the process to succeed participants need both to feel free to move between the elements in any direction and to be aware of the flow between their individual cycle and the encompassing group cycle.

Halprin's desire to create an inclusive dance ritual, *Circle the Earth*, that is meaningful to a wide a range of people and reflective of the diversity of the community entailed various choreographic challenges. While the RSVP process was sufficiently flexible to deal with the formidable task of producing a dance within a very short span of time (5–9 days) that satisfied participants on both an individual and community level, the question of the style of movement remained. In order to fulfil her stated intentions of creating 'dances that anybody can do' that would 'return people to an awareness of movement that I believe is one of our most essential birthrights' (Halprin with Kaplan 1995: 20), Halprin focused on the principle of encouraging participants to explore a wide range of movement responses within the structure of the score. Important to this inclusive stance was the learning of a common language through the use of 'natural, intrinsic movement', both to encourage everyone to dance and to focus on the way that '[t]he body's patterns reflect and influence the patterns of our lives' (Halprin with Kaplan 1995: 20) This allowed participants to engage with the work on a physical, emotional, intellectual and spiritual level and to create resources for the final performance. The performer's body was therefore valued for its holistic, idiosyncratic qualities rather than as a medium to be moulded into a preconceived aesthetic design.

THE *CIRCLE THE EARTH* SCORES

The prospect of running a week-long workshop culminating in a performance with over 100 people, many of whom have no background in dance, is daunting. However, Halprin had built up experience in the many large community dance classes and performances prior to the series. Years spent observing the recurrent patterns made by large groups moving in response to a range of instructions helped formulate the scores for *Circle the Earth*. These sustain a delicate balance, offering sufficient guidance to navigate safely through a potentially provocative process, without bringing into play a rigidity that would suffocate imaginative, physical and emotional response. In addition to allowing a great deal to be accomplished in a short time, the scores were sufficiently clear and flexible for those who had taken part in the ritual to use them as a basis for performing *Circle the Earth* in their own country/community. The rituals went 'on tour'. 'What travelled from place to place were not the performers or even a particular performance, but the scores, the recipes for creating the rituals' (Halprin 1995: 232).

The fact that *Circle the Earth* began with the scores already set and with some of those virtually closed, might seem to fly in the face of the idea of collective creativity. However, the scores act as a starting point to stimulate and channel the group's expression in the direction of an overall intention but without determining the end result. They help to structure the performance, but more importantly they are used extensively in the workshop to enable exploration of each theme through movement. Additions and alterations have been made to the scores in response to new participating groups, different environments or circumstances. The most extreme example was doing *Circle the Earth* 'at the American Dance Festival where most of the performers were professional dancers and used to strict choreography, we abandoned the *Circle the Earth* score and did an improvisation with Peace as the theme' (Halprin with Stinson 1987: 9).

In the course of describing her work, Halprin regularly refers to it as a craft that demands discipline. Although this differs in form from the demands of stylized step-based choreography, it takes no less rigour, time, energy and attention to detail to evolve. One example of this is evident in the balance achieved between 'open' and 'closed' scores within *Circle the Earth*, that determine the degree of freedom given to the participants in the instructions. A very closed score is one 'in which all the actions are defined and leave very little room for improvisation' (Halprin with Kaplan 1995: 23), while an open score contains instructions that encourage free movement exploration. The degree of openness of each score for *Circle the Earth* is shown on the outline below as a figure on a scale from 1 to 10, where 1 is open and 10 closed.

OUTLINE OF SCORES FOR *CIRCLE THE EARTH*

The scores for *Circle the Earth* mapped out below provide an idea of the overall structure of the performance. While the titles (with alternative names that occur in different versions of the dance shown in brackets) and intentions are taken directly from the 1987 manual produced for participants, the descriptions of activities are synopses of each section and are not taken verbatim from the text. Although there is an individual intention for each section, this is contained within an overarching aim for the whole performance: 'to make a vivid statement for mutual understanding and peace, one that can be taken from the performance in Marin and shared with many people in many places' (Halprin 1995: 244).

Score outline of *Circle the Earth*

Score 1: Preparation

'Every year we go to the mountain to reconnect with the natural world, to give thanks and receive blessings, to pray, to meditate and to celebrate' (Halprin with Stinson 1987: 14).

Score 2: I am the Earth (Rising and Falling)

Intention: To birth ourselves.

Participants begin lying in spirals and other forms then gradually rise from the earth to face the witnesses and request their support. *Scale*: 9.

Score 3: the Vortex (Snake dance)

Intention: To create a group identity.

From walking individually the group find a common pulse and evolve a dance that eventually uses vertical space to build an image, for instance a mountain. *Scale*: 2.

Score 4: Confrontation (Monster, Mask and Warrior dances)

Intention: To evoke and confront the destructive forces within us.

'Stomping rhythmically upon the ground, lines of warriors urge the monsters to emerge from the group. They enact for the performers and the witnesses the horror of death and destruction' (Halprin with Stinson 1987: 21). *Warriors' score – scale*: 9.5. *Monsters' score – scale*: 2.

The witnesses are asked to watch this section through white paper masks.

Score 5: Restoration

Intention: To heal our wounds and restore our lives.

To the singing of the restoration song the dancers hold and comfort each other, developing into contact movement. *Scale*: 3.

Score 6: Bridges and Passages

Intention: To create a pathway to peace.

The performers create a gateway and bridge through which they walk followed by the witnesses who may sing or dance. *Scale*: 5.

Score 7: the Earth Run

Intention: To make an offering to the planet. To voice and act on our commitment to peace.

The performers dedicate their run to a group or cause of their own choosing. They run in concentric circles, within a square of the four directions. 'The Earth run is a moving Mandala of Peace' (Halprin with Stinson 1987: 29). *Scale*: 9.

(This was originally known as the Chief Seattle Run due to the practice of reading his speech during the run. 'Back in 1853 Chief Seattle, of the Puget Sound Tribe wrote his reply to "the Great Chief in Washington" who had sought to acquire two million acres of land for $150,000' (Halprin with Stinson 1987: 31). However, this changed as *Circle the Earth* extended to other countries where this speech was substituted by poems or prose that held greater resonance for the local community.)

Score 8: Peace Wheel by Terry Riley (Sound Circle, Peace Song, Sound Spiral)

Intention: To create a wheel of harmony.

Singers at centre of a circle sing five different notes and turn slowly. The dancers in three concentric circles around them echo the different notes as the singers turn towards them. *Scale 9*.

Score 9: Bird Transformation

Intention: To send word of what has happened here to the whole planet.

Dancers spin out from the circles on the sound of the Peruvian whistles and didgeridoo and transform into their bird images. Closure of the dance with acknowledgement of witnesses and singing of the peace song. *Scale*: 5.

Score 10: Action and Commitment

Intention: To develop and communicate a personal programme to guide our actions for peace.

Participants write a statement on their intended action for peace. These are witnessed and reflected upon the following year.

Score 11: Peace Bird

Intention: To prepare for *The Planetary Dance* by uniting through a collective task.

At points during the workshop participants construct a Peace Bird for *The Planetary Dance*.

The final scores, 10 and 11, take place after the performance and do not appear in the same form in later versions. However, action and commitment is an essential part of the ritual and is always included in some format.

THE FUNCTION OF RSVP CYCLES: A DETAILED ANALYSIS OF TWO SCORES

The two scores selected below contrast sharply in construction and function within *Circle the Earth* and therefore provide an opportunity to explore the operation of the RSVP Cycles in relation to open and closed scoring. Since the workshops began with the scores set, as outlined above, the following analysis also starts from this point in the cycle. The aim is to expose the relationship between form and content in two scores, the 'Vortex' and the 'Earth Run', with particular emphasis on the dual function of each score to both provoke exploration and act as a container for the movement generated for the final performance.

The 'Vortex'

The 'Vortex' is the third and most open of the *Circle the Earth* scores and is presented in full below. An exceptionally dynamic use of the RSVP Cycles contributes to a dance, characterized by Halprin as 'the most fascinating dance to perform and witness, or the most perplexing, but always exciting and highly charged' (Halprin with Stinson 1987: 9).

THE VORTEX

INTENTION
To create a group identity.

THEME
In the Vortex Dance, we gather strength from each other. Using the ordinary movement of walking, we pass each other in the space in a kind of communal greeting. Within our different ways of walking, different paces and carriages, different steps and directions, we are searching for something: a common pulse, a common beat in the sounds of our feet upon the ground. Once we have

reached this non-verbal consensus, we build upon the group spirit it expresses. We dance in two's. We dance in three's. We build human families. Finally we join as a whole in the center of the space and build a symbol of our collective strength, a mountain.

ACTIVITIES

Walk.

Cooperate in finding a collective pulse.

Develop a personal walking movement to the collective pulse.

Evolve your dance.

Move in lines, circles, levels, areas, between, over, under, around.

Join and rejoin with other people, and other groups.

Build a mountain of people with a base and a peak in the center of the space. (The mountain image is changeable in accordance with each community's tradition – whatever is built needs to have a vertical use of space.)

TIME: 20 mins

SCALE: 2

(Halprin with Stinson 1987: 19)

S = score

The score for the 'Vortex' dance looks deceptively simple yet each activity releases new challenges for the participants. Its openness makes it 'the longest of all scores to practice, and invariably causes conflict as people struggle to make their own order out of chaos' (Halprin with Stinson 1987: 9). The following annotation is not comprehensive or prescriptive, it indicates questions and issues that might arise in doing the score and suggests how carefully these are raised in sequence to both provoke an energetic response and to provide sufficient security to support participation by all.

Intention: The 'chaos' arises early on, if not evident physically, then as an internal response to the intention for over 100 people to create a group identity. The dual provocative focus on group and individual identity remains at the heart of this score.

Theme: This outlines the type of content with which the dance is likely to engage.

Activities

Walk: For those daunted by the prospect of such an open score, the entry to the dance is reassuring. It is based on an everyday activity and, since there is no other specification, can be performed in any way the individual wishes. Although the simplicity of the action might act as a boost to confidence, the focus is on the self and the questions such as 'Who am I?' and 'Who am I in this context?' might begin to emerge and be expressed through the movement.

Co-operate: While still working with the same simple movement, this second instruction demands that the participants split their awareness between themselves and the group. This is a crucial point in the score and can take a long time since it requires non-verbal consensus. Questions about remaining true to oneself while co-operating with the whole group might be provoked.

Develop: If the sense of self has been subsumed within the collective, this instruction reignites the focus on individual movement. The common pulse is retained to unite and support the whole group, but each participant can find their own way of moving within it. This is a good example of Halprin's general guidance when working with scores to look at the gaps in the instructions that allow for creative freedom.

Evolve: This marks another critical point that needs individual and group confidence to move from walking into 'dance'. This could include participants redefining what dance is, or could be in response to what they witness. A wide range of movement resources is likely to emerge at this stage.

Move: More resources are added here to refresh the process and to deal consciously with the relationship to the environment and to the use of horizontal and vertical space, a process that could help broaden the perspective of the dancer in preparation for the final action.

Join: Particularly with such a large group the danger is that the group-ings can become stagnant as dancers fixate on one relationship or group. This instruction gives permission for participants to come and go in a free-flowing way. As in the previous action the intention is perhaps to remind participants of the broader perspective.

Build: The culmination of the score, dealing with community identity and group trust/co-operation.

P = performance

This term applies broadly to the enacting of a score in any context (workshop, ritual, theatrical). In the case of the 'Vortex', Halprin states that: 'We do the Vortex dance over and over throughout the workshop to develop our ability to be in improvisational space with one another' (Halprin with Kaplan 1995: 62). Valuaction between each performance leads to changes in resources or the score in order to avoid the problems of failure to build on improvisation. The final performance of the 'Vortex' in front of witnesses remains improvised. For this to be successful there is a need for an 'evolution of the collective's relationships, and the development of a rich movement language with one another' (Halprin with Kaplan 1995: 62). Although Halprin's aesthetic demand for the dance is secondary to the ritual purposes it pursues, the comment above raises the question of what entails 'success' in this context. She is concerned that the group can develop a rich movement language that is satisfying for the participants as well as being a means of conveying their experience to the witnesses.

The 'Vortex' dance is unusual in *Circle the Earth* since it is performed many times during the workshop, but all the workshop activities whether performance of the scores or exploration of resources lead towards the final performance. This has a significantly different quality from the previous performances that take place within the workshop context, since it is a distilled version of group intention and less focused on personal exploration. 'Performance is the enactment, or carrying out of the scores before the witnesses' and is the 'crystallization of 75 workshop hours into a two hour evening' (Halprin with Stinson 1987: 11).

V = valuaction

The coined word 'valuaction' brings together the process of evaluation and resulting action in a dynamic combination. This dual aspect is important as it fuels the movement onto the next stage of the RSVP Cycles. Where evaluation might suggest completion, 'valuaction' indicates a stage in a continuing process appropriate to the fluid relationship between the elements in the cycles. One participant in *Circle the Earth, Dancing with Life on the Line* described her pleasure in doing the dance in the following way: 'I was just there in the moment. I didn't think about what I was going to do. I didn't do anything I had planned to do'

(Halprin with Kaplan 1995: 63). Her relish of the immediacy and creative spontaneity experienced in this section of the dance is based on her acquiring the skills and discipline consistent with Halprin's description of her dance as a craft. The valuaction process of the RSVP Cycles ensures that the skills necessary for performing the score are elucidated and built upon. Participants might reflect on the specific elements of the dance that helped or hindered them as well as the overall demands of working in this open format. Practice therefore is not likely to be about achieving a certain series of steps as might be expected in a more stylized form. Instead the types of skills necessary would include: refining the dancers' awareness of their own movement in relation to a changing environment, staying alert to the intention, responding with flexibility to stimulus provided by other dancers and finding a balance between taking initiative and following a lead. Halprin confirms the importance of this particular combination in the following statement: 'The criterion I use to judge dances and the people who make them is both the conscious use of craft, and the artist's ability to make choices within that framework' (Halprin with Kaplan 1995: 29).

Halprin summarizes the valuaction process as being necessary in order to 'externalize, objectify and clarify the individual and group experience' resulting in improvement in the ability to 'build trust, make sense, support, co-operate, include input, make agreements, and resolve conflicts' (Halprin with Stinson 1987: 10).

The practical difficulties of achieving this degree of participation with such a large group are obvious. So a method of valuaction was set up for this and all other scores in *Circle the Earth* involving the establishment of small (seven to ten people) support groups. One person who had trained with Halprin or had particular skills took on the responsibility for feeding back a summary of the discussion to the facilitator. In this way each voice was heard and the facilitator could further summarize information in order to feedback to the whole group and 'assimilate it into the overall score, accommodating the group needs, discomforts, visions, suggestions and new ideas' (Halprin with Stinson 1987: 10). Different methods of valuaction were used by Halprin, the most common being: discussion in response to a series of direct questions, the use of visualization, partner work 'to practice being a witness and a performer' and experiments in small movement groups (Halprin with Stinson 1987: 10).

R = resources

There are many resources that have been included in the score such as choice of movements, motivation, space, number of people etc. The purpose of the workshop is for participants to individually find their connection to the resources offered. Just as the score is non-judgemental and does not say how it is to be accomplished or what the end result will look like, so too the resources do not include how any individual should feel. Although the resources from the score are explored on three levels of awareness (physical, emotional and images/content), specific emotions do not appear in lists of resources since this would destroy the immediacy of response that is essential in a dance ritual. Instead the action that provoked the feeling or image can be included in the score if appropriate. Of course certain movements or instructions are more likely than not to generate certain outcomes, but the success of the score is dependent on it remaining stimulating and meaningful for the participants.

RSVP Cycles

The daily repetition of the 'Vortex' dance is an example of rapid recycling from performance to valuaction and back into re-scoring or the addition of resources. The dance can be enriched through the recognition of the most helpful resources and through the refinement of the skills required by the dancers to accomplish the score. The subject matter and structure of the 'Vortex' clearly exposes the importance of the relationship between the personal and group cycles. 'Each score needs to have a personal meaning for the participant, but the dance as a whole must have a universal meaning for the witnesses and group as well' (Halprin with Stinson 1987: 10).

The 'Earth Run' score

If many of the *Circle the Earth* participants were daunted by the openness of the 'Vortex' score with subsequent demands on their own physical and imaginative response, there were others who were hesitant about the tight constraints evident in the 'Earth Run' score. The issues provoked are considered below, combined with a brief analysis of the score's structure. The colours mentioned under the section 'Activities' refers to the simple costuming of the different groups of dancers in white, black or rainbow colours.

THE EARTH RUN

INTENTION
To make an offering to the planet. To voice and act on our commitment to Peace.

THEME
We are part of the Earth. The Earth is part of us. Knowing this, we are also responsible to act upon it. Just as the Earth takes care of us, so we must take care of the Earth. The Earth Run is our act of commitment, an expression of our individual and collective dedication. We each run for a group of people on the earth of our own choosing: for a tribe or nation, a culture, a class, an ancestor, a loved one, for children, for the living, the dead, for those yet to be born. Run in concentric circles within the square of the four directions.

ACTIVITIES
Performers: Form a large circle in the space. Kneel.

Rainbow Colors begin the run. One by one stand and say 'I run for _____ (choose a group of people).'

Run counterclockwise within the large circle.

Run in a common pulse.

When all Rainbows are running, Black and White begin to join the running circle.

When you choose, run clockwise inside the first running circle.

When you choose, stop and stand facing one of the four directions.

You may rejoin the run or stand at any time.

Always change activities in sequence: (clockwise – counterclockwise – stand)

Never cut across lanes.

Stop wherever you are on the cue: 'Where is the thicket? Gone.' *[A line from the end of the 'Chief Seattle Speech']*

Witnesses: Voice your own dedications.

TEXT The Earth run is a moving Mandala of Peace.

       Each step upon the earth is a prayer for its healing.

(Chief Seattle Speech, or a narration of your community's choice.)

TIME: 20 mins

SCALE: 9

(Halprin with Stinson 1987: 29)

Score

In this seventh score the emphasis expands from the 'Vortex' content of individual in relation to immediate community, to community in relation to environment and planet. The running circles are neither inward looking, which represents self-sufficiency, nor outward looking to show the group relating outside themselves, but sideways on to allow 'the integration of the inner group itself with the outside world' (Halprin with Stinson 1987: 63). Unity of focus is encouraged through keeping the pulse and ensuring equal distance between all runners by altering pace to accommodate the shifting from one circle to another. The space is delineated with precision using the pattern of the circle contained by a square which 'represents balance, harmony and peace' (Halprin with Kaplan 1995: 99). Even within such a tightly structured score there is some room for individual variation as dancers choose which circle and therefore the speed to run at (the larger the circle the faster the speed to stay on the pulse) and how often they change circle.

Resources

The instructions for the dance are unusually prescriptive, providing specific suggestions for how dancers should run. This results in the preparation for the run looking closer to a traditional dance rehearsal than the free exploration of the 'Vortex'. For instance Halprin suggests that in order to emphasize the energetic connection between earth and sky, dancers need to run with an open chest, sternum forward and the torso straight with no wiggle or break at the pelvis (Halprin 2002b). Within the whole group aim of 'A prayer for peace among people and peace with the Earth' (Halprin and Planetary Dance Community 2002), each dancer calls out their own dedication that relates to a specific community or area of concern. This confirms an individual motivation in running while simultaneously marking the dance as the starting point in a commitment to action beyond the confines of the performance.

Performance

The ritual aspect of the performance is predominant in this score and extends to the formalized entry and exit from the running circles. Although the music and running can be energetic and joyful the intention is serious: that runners find the strength to go beyond their normal capacity through the support offered by the whole group, texts and music. In metaphoric terms this can be seen as recognition of the effort and commitment necessary to counteract violence and war as the favoured means of resolving conflict.

Valuaction

Unlike the 'Vortex' this dance is not repeated and refined through daily valuaction. Although the whole dance can be valuacted and has altered slightly over the years, the basic framework remains the same even when incorporated into *The Planetary Dance*. Logistical issues and specific performances can always be improved but perhaps the most significant element of valuaction lies in a more personal analysis. If the dance spans the transition from making a commitment within the group to sustaining that in the community then the valuaction process must similarly extend beyond the dance to address individual action after the performance.

Halprin is aware that the power generated by this form of dance can have its dangers as well as its strengths. She has worked over many years to provide 'safeguards' against the destructive forces evident in, for instance, cults or extreme political movements. 'By virtue of making a score (scenario) visible, learning and evaluating it, and them modifying it with their own images, the performers become empowered as co-creators of the dance' (Halprin 1995: 229). This reinforces the crucial role the RSVP Cycles have in the creation of these dance rituals and has repercussions for the style of leadership necessary that 'does not require obedience but rather creative involvement' (Halprin 1995: 229). After working on the 'Vortex', Halprin noticed: 'A larger power, a deep collective physical intelligence, directs the choreography. The more times these large group dances are done, the less outside direction is needed' (Halprin with Kaplan 1995: 62). In the 'Earth Run', by contrast, clear direction is needed before the dance and a very particular type of leadership is necessary once it has begun. Halprin's role then is as 'ritual keeper', the person who ensures that the small variations people introduce to stay alert to their dedication do not detract from the overall intention of the run.

The 'Earth Run' has somewhat different functions according to the context of its performance. When it is performed as part of *The Planetary Dance*, Halprin says: 'On the mountain, the Earth Run is the score we have to connect us to the mountain and to others doing this dance in other parts of the world' (Halprin with Kaplan 1995: 99). When the dance is done within the *Circle the Earth* performance in front of witnesses it 'is a step in the evolutionary process of healing' (Halprin with Kaplan 1995: 100).

DANCING WITH LIFE ON THE LINE AND THE FIVE STAGES OF HEALING

Circle the Earth, Dancing with Life on the Line (1989 and 1991) is the culmination of the previous ten years of exploration and holds a special significance for Halprin. Participants in *Dancing with Life on the Line* included people with HIV and AIDS, cancer and chronic fatigue. Their healing journey was the focus of the performances. The intention was 'to heal the fear, isolation and prejudice surrounding the AIDS crisis' (Halprin with Kaplan 1995: 12). This was 'a new version of Circle the Earth embodying a commitment to live' (Tamalpa Institute 1989). Halprin refers to the performance in 1989 as 'perhaps the most challenging, the most rewarding performance which I've experienced in my whole life . . . this is where my personal research and my competence was put to the test . . . this dance was the ultimate test of dance . . .' (Halprin 1995: 21). She also claims that this version of *Circle the Earth* was so changed that: 'You couldn't recognize it as the same dance' (Halprin 1995: 22).

In fact, most of the scores used to create the dance are the same as in earlier versions of *Circle the Earth*, with some striking and powerful new additions. However, the reality of the situation, coupled with the clarity and challenge of the intention, intensified the experience of the workshop and the performance. 'In a performance that utilizes the Life/Art Process, there is no need to playact or pretend. When you work with the real-life issues of the people who are performing, there is no abstraction, only real experience' (Halprin with Kaplan 1995: 28).

The particular achievement of *Dancing with Life on the Line* is the way in which it marries Halprin's work with life process and healing, with aesthetic concerns. It demonstrates her understanding and use of ritual in relation to performance and her unique approach to art-making through intense personal and group process.

In *Dancing with Life on the Line*, Halprin consciously uses the Five Stages of Healing process, which evolved out of her own experience of cancer, as 'the guiding choreographic structure for this dance' (Halprin 1995: 69). To use a process created for the purposes of healing as the artistic template for a performance ritual is a courageous undertaking. It is an example of Halprin's ability to cross boundaries and her skill in interweaving different concerns and layers of life experience. Her commitment to the quality and authenticity of the experience of her performers is unique and unwavering. At the same time she never loses sight of her artistic perspective, the fruit of all her years of experience in creating performance, of her long collaborations with other artists and her deeply ingrained sense of the body in motion and in relationship to space. She is clear that: 'Both the efficacy and the craft of Circle the Earth are important to me' (Halprin with Kaplan 1995: 29). *Dancing with Life on the Line* demonstrates unequivocally that she is no longer interested in creating art for art's sake but in 'dancing the dance that is needed' (Halprin with Kaplan 1995: 30).

THE FIVE STAGES OF HEALING

In *Dancing with Life on the Line*, Halprin used the process of the Five Stages of Healing in conjunction with the RSVP Cycles. The RSVP Cycles provided a framework for generating collective creativity and a common language with which to communicate. The Five Stages of Healing offered a map for the healing journey undertaken both by individuals and the community.

The seeds for this map grew out of Halprin's transformative experience of dancing her self-portrait when she was struggling with cancer in the early 1970s. As she reflected on this experience and began to articulate her approach to working with others, she became aware that her experience was relevant to the healing process in general. She has continued to apply this process in her work with dance and healing. Her daughter Daria Halprin Khalighi has developed this approach as the Five Part Process in the context of expressive arts therapy (Halprin Khalighi 1989: 46–61).

For Halprin the Five Stages of Healing

> constitute a 'rite of passage,' a series of activities that mark moments of signif-
> icance in a person or a community's life. Traditionally, rites of passage
> acknowledge the passage of time – birth, death, entrance to adulthood, and
> marriage are all marked by rites of passage . . . . My self-portrait and my dance

were a personal rite of passage; Circle the Earth is a rite of passage for an entire community.

(Halprin with Kaplan 1995: 17)

The Five Stages of Healing are:

1   Identification.
2   Confrontation.
3   Release.
4   Change (sometimes referred to as Integration or Transformation).
5   Assimilation (also referred to as Growth or Application).

Identification names the issue or theme to be addressed, which is the focus of the ensuing process. In *Dancing with Life on the Line* the core issue was life and death.

Confrontation is the physical enactment/embodiment of the feelings and images associated with this life issue.

Release involves a physical, emotional and mental letting go, as a result of the expression elicited in the stage of confrontation. It opens the way to the next stage of healing.

Change constitutes an integration of what has happened, a transformation from 'one state of being to another', a new way of perceiving oneself and of being in the world.

Assimilation is the application of the knowledge or experience gained in daily life.

(adapted from Halprin with Kaplan 1995: 16–17
and Halprin Khalighi 1989: 46–56)

Each of the scores in *Dancing with Life on the Line*, both in the performance and in the preparatory workshop, can be located within these five stages. The divisions between the stages are not rigid and they may overlap. Anna and Daria Halprin point out that the process is not necessarily linear and can involve starting at different points or returning to earlier stages. However, the later stages of Change and Assimilation cannot effectively take place without the earlier stages.

When examining *Dancing with Life on the Line* from the perspective of the Five Stages of Healing it is essential to address the process in its entirety rather than just the performance. The performance was the climax of the healing journey undertaken by the participants in the workshop. The order in which the scores were explored and developed during the workshop was not necessarily the order in which they were performed. The final stages of the healing process, Change and Assimilation, continued after the performance on the day of closure, in follow-up meetings and in the participants' daily lives. During the workshop each of the performance scores was explored in depth, accompanied by careful preparation and creative process, both individually and in the group. Simply rehearsing and performing prescribed scores is not only alien to Halprin's approach to creativity but also would not have functioned effectively as a healing journey for the participants.

At the beginning of the workshop before embarking on the first stage of the healing process the group was taken through a number of preparatory scores. These included drawing self-portraits and exploratory movement scores and games to establish trust and prepare the group for working together in depth. The second day was spent on the mountain where the group participated in *The Planetary Dance* experiencing the 'Earth Run' in the environment before recreating it in the performance.

Below the performance scores are identified in relation to their function in the Five Stages of Healing. Scores of particular significance in *Dancing with Life on the Line* are examined in more detail.

IDENTIFICATION

In *Dancing with Life on the Line* the two scores which belong to this first stage of healing are 'I am the Earth' and the new score 'I Want to Live'.

'I am the Earth'

'I am the Earth', also referred to as 'Rising and Falling', has always reflected the cycle of life and death in *Circle the Earth*. In *Dancing with Life on the Line* it took on a new resonance. Halprin guides the participants through a detailed kinaesthetic exploration of rising and falling using the movements to metaphorically confront the core theme of life and death. Participants are encouraged to connect with the personal images, feelings and associations evoked by this exploration. Given the nature of the group this was particularly confronting and served as a way of defying a cultural avoidance of death, and the taboo of expressing our feelings about it. I am the Earth is a commitment for all of us, dancing alone and in a group, to get in touch with where we stand in regard to life and death, and to make our own offering.

(Halprin with Kaplan 1995: 53)

This is a period of personal preparation and research. As the participants explore, and witness each other exploring, rising and falling, they are extending their movement resources not in order to choreograph their performance, but to deepen their feeling connection to the material. 'In this exercise, the performer isn't asked to pretend or re-enact, but to feel their experience of living or dying in that moment, to "practise" living and dying' (Halprin with Kaplan 1995: 52). This is a clear example of the double spiral, central to the Life/Art Process, of deepened life experience married with expanded artistic expression (Halprin 1995: 15). The discussions that followed these explorations were passionate, personal and revealingly honest. Halprin's associations of rising with life and falling with death were challenged by the experiences of the group. Her commitment as facilitator of the group healing process, as well as director of the performance, is to agree upon a version of the score which allows each individual to connect with their personal experience of the theme in an authentic way. The movement explorations were followed by journal writing and creative visualizations on the theme of life and death. These, combined with sharing in small support groups, allowed the participants the time and space to begin to integrate their experiences and to see them in relation to the 'larger myth' (Halprin with Kaplan 1995: 56). That is to locate the personal within the context of an exploration of the human condition. Personal material is respected and is central to the content of the performance within the framework of a larger score that provides both an artistic structure and the matrix for the healing ritual. It is not manipulated for Halprin's artistic aims, nor used as a way of simply generating theatrical material.

'I Want to Live'

This score was developed in response to a crisis in the group during the workshop process. The crisis highlighted the fact that the participants with life-threatening illness were directly engaged in a fight for their lives and the others weren't. A crisis in the group dynamic and the artistic process, it threatened to split the group and epitomized the challenges of the type of theatre Halprin creates with 'raw and human experiences calling for immediate resolution through new and creative means' (Halprin with Kaplan 1995: 57). The crisis was catalysed when a participant shockingly admitted his jealousy of the group members with HIV, claiming they were the stars of the show. The score that Halprin evolved to address this issue was simple and direct. It focused on the common ground that all the participants shared, their desire for life. Each person was invited to walk or run down a pathway formed by other members of the group and to say 'I want to live' as they approached the witnesses. This bald statement stripped bare the core issue which the group was grappling with and confronted the partici-pants directly with their feelings about life and death. The experience of carrying out the score returned the group to the original intention of *Dancing with Life on the Line* providing an emotional and artistic reso-lution to the crisis that threatened to undermine the project.

'I Want to Live' simultaneously provided new and powerful per-formance material. In earlier versions of *Circle the Earth*, performers had come forward announcing their names and countries (Halprin with Stinson 1987: 17). In *Dancing with Life on the Line*, the participants with HIV, AIDS-related conditions and AIDS made themselves visible before a thousand witnesses affirming their desire for life. It is a riveting moment even on video (*Circle the Earth: Dancing with Life on the Line* 1989) because they are fighting for their lives and because of their per-sonal courage in refusing invisibility and the challenge that this presents to the community. For some performers it radically changed their atti-tude to being visible with their HIV status in their daily lives (Halprin with Kaplan 1995: 120).

This score works theatrically because of the performers' authenticity and because it confronts the witnesses directly with the content of the performance. For the same reasons it works for the performers as a significant step in their healing journey:

> When it was my turn, when I said, 'My name is David and I want to live,' I really meant it. It wasn't a performance. It wasn't a dance. It was the first time in my life I consciously said, 'I want to live'. And it was the first time since I had been diagnosed with AIDS I had consciously said 'I want to live' and meant it. This was the most powerful moment for me in the dance.
>
> (Halprin with Kaplan 1995: 59)

Figure 3.4 *Circle the Earth* rocks hanging in the gym. Photograph by Jay
          Graham

The two scores, 'I am the Earth' and 'I Want to Live', make the
theme and intention of *Dancing with Life on the Line* clear. They form the
first step of the healing journey, Identification, as well as being the opening scores of the performance. The group is now poised to move
towards the second stage of confrontation.

CONFRONTATION

The new score 'Tell the Truth' and the 'Monster/Mask and Warrior'
dances constitute the confrontation stage in *Dancing with Life on the Line*
(Halprin with Kaplan 1995: 62–76).

The 'Vortex' dance which takes place between these two scores
prepares the ground, providing a strong enough sense of community to
contain the extreme emotions that are provoked by the 'Monster and
Warrior' dances:

> the Vortex dance is done in preparation for our confrontation with illness and
> death. . . . The group needed all the strength, power and affirmation it could
> mobilize before taking on the arduous task of facing and confronting its demons.
>
> (Halprin with Kaplan 1995: 62)

'Tell the Truth'

Like 'I Want to Live', the new 'Tell the Truth' score was developed in response to the difficulties within the group and addresses the central issues of *Dancing with Life on the Line*. In this score, participants with HIV call a member of the group out to support them, telling them why they have chosen them. In the workshop the score, which only evolved fully on the morning of the performance, facilitated the speaking of many powerful and hidden truths. Like 'I Want to Live', it was highly emotional and confrontational, and served to heighten the commitment of the group to the process and to each other. Halprin sees these two scores as 'the signature scores of Dancing with Life on the Line. They are the movement portraits of the group self' (Halprin with Kaplan 1995: 65).

Out of the context it may appear that this score has more in common with the revelations of confessional chat shows on daytime television or group therapy than performance. Witnessing the process it becomes clear that the integrity with which it is performed and experienced has little to do with sensational confessions or emotional voyeurism (*Circle the Earth: Dancing with Life on the Line* 1989). Instead it enables the group to move onto the next stage of healing, breaking through some of the barriers of isolation, fear and prejudice surrounding HIV. Like the 'Vortex' score, but using radically different means, it strengthens the sense of community. In effect it mirrors the process that needs to happen in the larger community in the context of the performance group. For Halprin, the authenticity demanded by this score in performance is essentially a performance skill (Halprin with Kaplan 1995: 65). 'Tell the Truth' retains its power in performance precisely because the performers are still in touch with the raw feelings it provokes rather than attempting to re-enact them.

The 'Monster' dance

This score together with the 'Warrior' dance forms the core of the Confrontation stage of the healing process. The intention of these scores is 'to release the destructive forces' (Halprin with Kaplan 1995: 74). In earlier versions of *Circle the Earth* this was related to war, violence or destruction of the environment depending on the theme of the particular year. In *Dancing with Life on the Line* the demon was the 'killer within' of the AIDS virus.

Confrontation is the most demanding part of the personal process. Participants are carefully prepared for the score in order to ensure that it functions as a healing catharsis rather than a destructive provocation without resolution. Before entering the exploration of their personal monsters participants are led through a healing meditation which connects them to a 'sacred healing place in nature' (Halprin with Kaplan 1995: 71). This meditation prefigures the 'Restoration' score in the performance. For Halprin this is an essential safeguard because of the level of emotional process that the 'Monster' dance provokes. It demonstrates her clear sense of responsibility towards the participants and her concern for their psychological safety:

> In preparing to plunge into the dark side of anger, fear and anguish, it is imperative to first secure three things: a safe and strong place within; a way to maintain yourself through darkness; and a place where you can return.
>
> (Halprin with Kaplan 1995: 70)

These are broadly therapeutic concerns that are also necessary to create a successful rite of passage. Nevertheless the resulting performance score is highly dramatic, constructed to ensure that the urgency and power of the conflict is communicated to the witnesses.

In the workshop the resources for the 'Monster' dance are researched through a combination of kinaesthetic explorations and drawn visualizations. The face itself is used as a mask. Participants are encouraged to explore the 'mask' that connects them most powerfully to their 'dark' side and to embody this in dance. To this end intensity and extremity in images and movements are encouraged (Halprin with Kaplan 1995: 69). In the workshop all the participants explore the confrontation with their own monsters so that it is a healing process for everyone. As 'ritual keeper' Halprin decided that in the performance only the participants with life threatening illnesses would dance the monsters because of their ongoing struggle with the forces of destruction (Halprin with Kaplan 1995: 75).

In the performance the facial masks discovered in the workshop process are used as a way of re-triggering the emotions provoked during the earlier explorations. Most of the participants are not trained performers and would not have the performance skills to enact the intense emotions generated by the 'Monster' dance. The score is constructed to allow them to experience the feelings and to embody them in the dance.

This is Halprin's skill in working with untrained performers. More technical working methods would not be as successful artistically with such a group nor would they serve the participants in their healing process.

After the 'Vortex' dance the build up to the 'Monster' score sets the emotional tenor for the dance preparing both the performers and witnesses. The narrator rallies the group from their positions on the floor by a repetitive drumbeat and a chant that swells as the participants join him:

> OUT! OUT! OUT! OUT!
> We're drawing the line
> Our lives are on the line
> OUT! OUT! OUT! OUT!
> (Halprin with Kaplan 1995: 74)

The witnesses are included in the score for the 'Monster' dance in an action which serves both a theatrical and ritual purpose. Plain white masks of various shapes had been placed on each seat. Prior to the dance the narrator urged the witnesses to hold the masks in front of their faces: 'Witnesses, put on your masks. We need to be protected when the warrior lines come forward pushing the danger out. Witnesses, put on your masks. We need to be protected when the carriers break through carrying the poison out' (Halprin with Kaplan 1995: 76).

From the perspective of the ritual there is a belief that a negative force is being expelled in the 'Monster' dance and therefore a genuine need to protect the witnesses from receiving the full impact of the energy that is being directed towards them (Halprin with Kaplan 1995: 75–6). The masks serve to distance the audience from the intensity of the emotion being expressed, paradoxically perhaps allowing them to receive it more fully without the need to distance themselves in other ways. As the dancers approach the witnesses their experience is intensified by this unexpected wall of white masks and they in turn are protected from any emotional reaction on the part of the witnesses.

The 'Warrior' dance

The 'Warrior' dance is performed by the rest of the group simultaneously to the 'Monster' score. The function of the warriors is to support the monster dancers and to give them strength and energy

(Halprin with Kaplan 1995: 73) to embody their monsters fully in performance. The monster dancers have also experienced the power of dancing their warriors. In the performance the warriors embody that power for them so that they are not overwhelmed by the symbolic forces with which they are struggling. In turn the warriors are able to empathize with the experience of the monster dancers.

The 'Warrior' dance is the most dynamic score in *Circle the Earth* and it is an unusually closed score. Whereas the 'Monster' dance is concerned with the struggle of the individual, the 'Warrior' dance represents the power of the collective. Both the movements used and the spatial patterns of the dance are prescribed. The warriors advance in unison in lines which the monsters break through; using an 'insistent' beat the warriors lift their legs in a 'high-stepping movement' to the side, using their voices as they bring them down forcefully on the downbeat with the chest raised (Halprin with Kaplan 1995: 73). This choreographic framework, effective in performance terms, was chosen because of its function in the healing process. The movements are an affirmation of the strength necessary to confront the challenges of the situation.

Halprin maintains that certain movements or movement qualities can engender certain feelings, but she is clear that it is not possible to score feelings directly. Although the movements of the 'Warrior' dance are prescribed, it was crucial, both for ritual and artistic purposes, that the dancers experienced the movements on a personal level; that the three levels of awareness, physical, emotional and mental, were fully engaged. Some participants initially had difficulty in embodying the movements in the 'Warrior' dance, but as they were challenged to broaden their movement vocabulary they also experienced a sense of personal empowerment (Halprin with Kaplan 1995: 73 and 85). This is another example of interlocking spirals of the Life/Art Process: 'When participants viscerally experience the Warrior movements, there is a marked visual change. . . . It is precisely because of its transformative quality that this particular movement was chosen' (Halprin with Kaplan 1995: 73).

Alongside the clarity of this intention Halprin's aesthetic sense is also clearly operating in the dynamic of the movement, and the use of space and colour as the lines of warriors, each in a different rainbow colour, advance towards the witnesses.

In the final section of this score the warriors embody victory over the forces of destruction and move forward to comfort the monster dancers in the dance of 'Restoration'.

RELEASE

After the intensity of the confrontation the 'Restoration' score provides a change of atmosphere and pace. It is a time of recuperation necessary for performers and witnesses alike and constitutes the third stage of the healing process: Release. The performers are physically and emotionally exhausted after the 'Monster' dance, leaving them vulnerable and receptive to the care and gentle touch offered by other members of the group. This is a movement from isolation to compassion. One participant describes it as 'a kind of rebirth' (Halprin with Kaplan 1995: 90). Halprin comments that this sense of connection was mirrored among the witnesses, some of whom spontaneously reached out to one another (Halprin with Kaplan 1995: 88).

The narration of the 'Restoration' poem and song (which continues during the 'Bridge' score), with its repeated phrases and simple harmonies, is reminiscent of a litany and is imbued with spiritual resonance. In this struggle between life and death 'The promise of life is restored' (Halprin with Kaplan 1995: 92).

For Halprin the 'Bridge' provides the transition from Release, to the stage of Change in the healing process:

> People are beginning to resolve their own personal issues of grief and loss and are able to attend to the grief and loss of the collective body. There is a newfound ability to connect to the larger world of humanity, to recognize the universality of suffering and the possibility of change . . . .
>
> (Halprin with Kaplan 1995: 90)

CHANGE

Several different scores, together with the final day of the workshop after the performance, form the fourth stage of the healing process: Change.

The 'Earth Run'

The 'Earth Run', the structure of which has been discussed earlier, is central to this process of change:

> This is the moment when we can begin to see new options both in our beliefs and our behaviors. We have recognized our circumstances, named them, grieved them. Now we have the opportunity to stand in a new relationship to them.
>
> (Halprin with Kaplan 1995: 99)

In an integration of the earlier stages of the Five Part Process there is a progression from affirming the individual's will to live, to affirming the life of others and of the planet.

The 'Sound Spiral' and 'Victory' dance

The 'Sound Spiral', which is an evolution from the 'Peace Wheel' and the 'Bird Transformation' in earlier versions of *Circle the Earth*, also forms part of the stage of Change, or Transformation. Both scores 'are associated with new growth and new beginnings' (Halprin with Kaplan 1995: 100). The 'Spiral' dance symbolically links the participants to the wider world as they spiral out from the centre of the space. The 'Victory' score invites the witnesses, starting with those most closely affected by life-threatening illness, to join the dancers and to sing the 'Restoration' song. The closed community of participants who shared the intense ritual journey is widened to include the community of their daily lives.

Closure

The day after the performance the group met to complete their process together. Halprin was conscious of the need for the participants to make a transition from ritual time and space to everyday life. The emphasis was on integrating the experiences of the previous week and the performance on a conscious level. Participants were guided through a reflective process that facilitated 'a metaphoric reading of the experience as a way to apply the lessons we learned through dance to our daily lives' (Halprin with Kaplan 1995: 100). This enabled them to understand the changes that had taken place as a result of participating in *Dancing with Life on the Line*, and to make choices based on these experiences in the future. A return from the collective experience to personal learning, this process clarified the relationship between the individual and collective mythologies engendered. Self-portraits, which had been used on the first day of the workshop, were used again giving the participants an external representation of the result of their healing journey. The workshop closed with a prayer and a return to nature, this time the ocean, for a feast and celebration.

ASSIMILATION

The fifth and final stage of the process, Assimilation, happened for the participants after the workshop, as the repercussions of their experiences during this intensive period reverberated through their lives. Halprin acknowledges that the process of assimilation 'often takes a long and circuitous path' (Halprin with Kaplan 1995: 130). Since many of the performers facing HIV were part of the Steps Theatre Company and Women with Wings these participants continued to have contact both with one another and with Halprin. These groups also had their own closure ceremonies as part of their process of integration and transition. Through her continuing contact with participants Halprin was aware of some of the ways in which individuals applied the experience gained in their lives.

Inevitably after such a heightened experience and with the challenges of living with life-threatening illness the transitions were not always smooth. Halprin describes the struggle of the Women with Wings group to come to terms with the deterioration in the health of one of their members who had been hospitalized during the workshop. For Halprin the fact that the group had the resources to face the negative and self-destructive feelings evoked by this situation together and ultimately found a spontaneous resolution was indicative of how much they had gained (Halprin with Kaplan 1995: 109–10).

According to Halprin the experience of *Dancing with Life on the Line* left many participants better equipped to face the challenges of their daily lives:

Many participants in the workshop acknowledged afterwards that the tools they had gained – access to their bodies, the resource of their visual images, and the mental and spiritual associations these realms held for them – were tools they could integrate into their daily lives and use over and over again. The processes of reclaiming the symbols of the body and the mind serves participants long after the dance has ended.

(Halprin with Kaplan 1995: 108–9)

Halprin makes a distinction between curing and healing, she does not suggest that the Five Part Process is a way of curing people but rather a holistic approach to healing.

To 'cure' is to physically eliminate a disease . . . . To 'heal' is to operate on many dimensions simultaneously, by aiming at attaining a state of emotional, mental, spiritual and physical health. Healing also addresses the psychological dimension and works with belief systems, whether they are life-enhancing or

> destructive. It is possible, therefore, that a person with a terminal diagnosis
> may not be cured, but can be healed, and inversely, that someone can be cured,
> but not healed.
>
> (Halprin 2000: 15)

In these terms *Dancing with Life on the Line* (1989) served as an effective healing ritual for the participants.

RITUAL OR PERFORMANCE?

Throughout the above discussion the use of the word ritual recurs, so how are we to view *Circle the Earth* and specifically *Dancing with Life on the Line*? Is it ritual or performance? What is the relationship between the two?

Dancing with Life on the Line never masquerades simply as a theatre performance. Every element of how it is described, created and performed is infused with another layer of intention. This does not invalidate it as performance but reminds us that it cannot be viewed solely from a theatrical perspective. There is another agenda, in addition to an artistic one, and any assessment of the work must take this other dimension into account. It is inappropriate to discuss or critique *Dancing with Life on the Line* solely, or even primarily, on the basis of its merit as theatre. This does not mean that it can be dismissed as a ritual that has no place in a discussion of contemporary performance. We have seen earlier that Halprin is a child of her time and the cultural environments within which her work has evolved. A maverick child perhaps but, precisely because of this, one whose influence has permeated contemporary performance practice more widely than is generally acknowledged. It is too easy to marginalize work such as Halprin's that challenges and crosses boundaries because it defies tidy classification, upsetting established or fashionable notions of dance and performance.

Halprin is uninterested in an academic discussion of the boundaries of ritual and performance. As a practitioner who reflects on her practice her approach is a fundamentally pragmatic one: 'Something that is a ritual is not necessarily art, and vice versa, but it is always my intention to create an artful ritual' (Halprin with Kaplan 1995: 28). For her performances such as *Circle the Earth* effectively 'blur the boundaries between art and ritual as they exist in our contemporary culture' (Halprin with Kaplan 1995: 29). This implies these boundaries are to some extent arbitrary, have been variously delineated in other times or in non-western (for example, indigenous) cultures and are dependent on a changeable definition of the terms involved.

For Halprin the most important characteristic of a ritual is that it carries the specific intention of creating change and that it connects with a higher power, with something larger than ourselves (Halprin with Kaplan 1995: 28). A ritual is therefore imbued with spiritual resonance. All the decisions made during the process of creating *Dancing with Life on the Line* are congruent with the intention in creating this ritual. Halprin is acutely aware of the difference between the workshop process which is essentially 'a personal and inward experience' and the performance which is 'an outward and community orientated event' and the difficulties inherent in this transition for the group (Halprin with Kaplan 1995: 116). She is not interested in creating entertainment or images for their own sake. She *is* concerned with creating a ritual that involves the witnesses with the life and death issues that the participants are facing. Authenticity is primary not only in terms of process but also artistically. Halprin uses her artistic sensibilities to channel and structure the experiences of the dancers so that they serve not only their individual needs but also those of the group and communicate effectively to the larger community. As an artist she is keenly aware that the form in which the work is expressed is fundamental to its ability to fulfil its intention:

> The gap between 'art' and 'ritual' can be traversed when we are conscious not only of the content of the work and its effects on the participants, but also the form and manner in which this content is presented. It is my . . . highest ideal in the creation and use of the Life/Art Process to make rituals that are art, and to make art that is ritualistic in nature.
>
> (Halprin with Kaplan 1995: 30)

One reviewer of the first mountain performance was critical of Halprin's attempts to present ritual in a theatrical context (Ross 1981). Halprin herself didn't feel these performances worked (Halprin 1995: 21 and 24). Their weakness was that the relatively conventional theatrical form and setting served neither the content nor the underlying intention. In the evolution of *Circle the Earth* the two strands of art and ritual become so closely interwoven as to be inseparable. With *The Planetary Dance*, community ritual supersedes performance altogether.

RITUAL TIME

Halprin works consciously with notions of ritual time and space, differ-
entiating them from both daily life and performance. In many ways
the workshop has more in common with a liminal period, when those
who are to take part in a ritual are removed from the circumstances of
their daily lives and undergo an intensive period of preparation, than it
does with conventional rehearsals for performance. During this period
participants are prepared: physically, emotionally, mentally and spiri-
tually. They are given the knowledge and the skills necessary to undergo
what is required of them. The careful preparation of the dancers for
the 'Monster' dance, ensuring that the participants are both personally
equipped to face the emotional demands of the experience and are safely
contained within the context of the larger group, bring to mind the
preparations of participants in other sacred rites. The timing of this
score, preceded by the strengthening experience of community in the
'Vortex' dance and followed by the nurturing of the 'Restoration', is
dictated by the needs of the ritual rather than by theatrical structure.
As an experienced 'elder', Halprin is concerned, and takes responsibility for, the well-being of those undergoing this rite of passage but
within the containing structure of the ritual she is uncompromising
about the demands made on them. These demands are governed by the
underlying intention of the ritual and by her experience of, and belief
in, the efficacy of the Five Part Process, rather than the artistic imper-
atives of most directors. The 'Victory' dance, in which the witnesses
merge with performers, breaks notions of western theatrical time and
continues for more than an hour.

RITUAL SPACE

The preparation of the space is also governed more by the demands of
ritual than by those of theatre. The gym was transformed from a secular
to a 'sacred' space by the participants creating altars of fruit and flowers
in the four directions. Halprin uses religious terms such as altar, prayer
and sacred, loosely without affiliation to a particular religion, allowing
room for participants to imbue them with their own meaning. For
Halprin, the altars bring beauty into the space and evokes nourishment,
marking 'the life spirit' (Halprin with Kaplan 1995: 115) and reminding
participants that they are working with the cycle of life and death. As
part of their preparation participants were encouraged to visit the altars

and to meditate. The group also received the blessings of spiritual leaders in the community to remind the dancers of the ritual intention of the performance, and its relationship to 'a higher power' and to the wider community. The blessings of spiritual leaders (both indigenous and western), together with honouring the four directions, has been an ongoing feature of the dance since 1981 and continues in *The Planetary Dance*.

The rocks which are suspended from the ceiling as part of the 'set' in *Dancing with Life on the Line* create an evocative theatrical environment, simultaneously beautiful, powerful and precarious, but they also function on a symbolic level. Each participant searched for a rock the size of their skull and brought it to the studio. Through the course of the workshop the rocks became imbued with personal symbolic meaning, functioning 'as a container for the feelings, fantasies, insights, dreams and associations that are generated during the workshop' (Halprin with Kaplan 1995: 44). The participants' relationship with their rock continued to evolve beyond the duration of the workshop and performance. The performers emerge from the rocks in the truth-telling score which could be interpreted as symbolizing both the personal and theatrical risks inherent in this score and the weightiness of the truths involved. Just as the participants had different names and associations for the environment created by the rocks they will have evoked different images and emotions for the witnesses.

It is important that the participants were actively involved with the creation of the altars and the selection of the rocks, enabling them to find their own relationship to these symbolic elements. Other symbolic objects such as the eagle feathers, which are run through the space at the opening of the performance, gain significance from their repeated use in *Circle the Earth* and *The Planetary Dance* and the stories associated with them as part of the 'Living Myth':

> A ritual contains within it specific symbols which are made meaningful to members of the community through repetition and the creation of a common language which invests these symbols with significance. The input of the collective is crucial in the creation and maintenance of a ritual.
>
> (Halprin with Kaplan 1995: 28)

At the opening of *Dancing with Life on the Line* the witnesses are led into the ritual space through a 'pathway of light' (Halprin with Kaplan

1995: 115). These lighted candles had been placed by each of the performers in memory of someone who had died. They served as a memorial, highlighting the theme of life and death, and linking the dancers and witnesses.

WITNESSES

Halprin's concept of witnesses is fundamentally different from that of a theatre audience. They are participants in the ritual with a specific function and responsibilities; they are there neither to judge nor to be entertained but to witness and support the participants' rite of passage. The witnesses for *Dancing with Life on the Line* were prepared for the ritual separately from the performers and before entering the performance space. They were informed of the process that the participants had been through and that their reason for performing was 'to make themselves visible, it is important for them, they're not doing it for you, they're doing it because they want to claim their pride, their courage and their nobility and . . . you will be their witnesses' (*Circle the Earth: Dancing with Life on the Line* 1989).

To be a witness requires an element of receptivity but it is not a passive role; their presence is crucial to the effectiveness of the ritual. Rather than the distance of a spectator their personal involvement is invited. In the preparation before the performance of *Dancing with Life on the Line* the witnesses were encouraged 'to meditate on what in themselves they wanted to be healed, and for whom among their friends and families they wished to pray' (Halprin with Kaplan 1995: 115–16).

There were three layers of healing operating in *Dancing with Life on the Line*, firstly the personal healing journey that has been described in depth. The wider purpose was to heal the fear, prejudice and ignorance surrounding AIDS in the community. During the workshop these issues were addressed within the group. In the truth-telling score an honest dialogue between those with HIV and AIDS and the other participants was initiated, feelings of isolation and the fear of rejection and exhaustion were revealed, attitudes such as the fear of infection and moral judgements were owned and transformed. Through this process and the shared experiences of the workshop and performance, acceptance and increased trust were engendered. The performance became a means of spreading this ripple of change out into the wider community:

> to reach out to our extended community in a way that would encourage a
> trusting, loving and non-prejudiced viewing of the participants' lives. We
> needed witnesses to clarify our intention to heal, and we hoped to create an
> event that would enable people with HIV to be accepted, without judgement,
> by their community.
>
> (Halprin with Kaplan 1995: 114)

The intention was to affect the attitudes and beliefs of the witnesses, so that they too underwent change as a result of participating in the ritual. The measures taken to ensure the safe passage of the dancers through this ritual were mirrored in the treatment of the witnesses. They were prepared beforehand and their transition into ritual time and space was symbolically marked. They were symbolically protected from potential psychic harm through the use of the white masks. At the completion of the ritual those witnesses most likely to have been directly affected by it were invited into the centre of the ritual space and participated in the 'Restoration' song. Then the circle was extended to include all the witnesses. As the witnesses merged with the performers the ethos of the workshop was also extended to them; there was time, space and permission for physical contact, the expression of feelings, dance and celebration.

Since many of the witnesses had close relationships with the participants they were deeply affected by the ritual. One dancer chose to use the performance as a way of telling his family of his HIV status. Identified as HIV positive through his participation in the 'I Want to Live' score, his family's journey as witnesses mirrored his own, through shock, grief, restoration and celebration. The ritual left them 'with a feeling of strength, support and faith' (Halprin with Kaplan 1995: 61). For them too it was a healing ritual.

Halprin draws comparisons between *Circle the Earth* and the rituals of some non-western cultures, for example the Andaman Islands (Halprin with Stinson 1987: 74) and Bali (Halprin with Kaplan 1995: 87). She gives examples of the use of masks in these cultures and suggests a parallel between the trance states entered by masked dancers in a Balinese ritual she attended and the altered state of the performers in the 'Monster' dance. Halprin has attended many indigenous rituals, including a powerful and confronting experience witnessing the Native American Sun Dance in 1989 (Halprin with Kaplan 1995: 80). While these experiences have informed her understanding of her own work in creating rituals, she does not claim them as sources and, as already noted, has no wish to appropriate the rituals of other cultures. She acknowledges that in comparison with such traditional and stylized rituals *Circle the Earth* is 'raw' and 'unrefined' (Halprin with Kaplan 1995: 87). For Halprin one of the features of such contemporary rituals is that they are necessarily 'multi-dimensional' since they do not represent one cultural group (Halprin 2002a).

Halprin's approach to ritual is essentially idealistic and dynamic, she believes in the power of contemporary, dance rituals to address problematic social and environmental issues in our society, to change the way we live, individually and collectively:

> I see us dancing the hard dances until they become easy, stumbling and tripping over each other until we learn to dance together. I see it all as a wonderful possibility and a great hope . . . hoping that the process that created Circle the Earth will encourage the creation of all the dances we need to learn to live gracefully with one another and the planet that supports us.
>
> (Halprin with Kaplan 1995: 131)

4

PRACTICAL
EXPLORATIONS

INTRODUCTION

This chapter provides resources for an experiential exploration of Halprin's approach. The suggestions that follow will give the reader an opportunity to develop a more embodied understanding of Halprin's work and allow a deeper understanding of the ideas and working methods discussed previously.

Scores used by Halprin are included in this chapter with her permission; these are clearly marked. Other sequences are inspired by training with Halprin and have been devised to illuminate particular aspects of her work; they include applications of the processes with which she works. Since Halprin's work is based on process, enduring aspects of her work have evolved throughout the course of her career. They have been presented and applied differently at different stages in this evolution and are continuing to evolve. It must be stressed therefore that Halprin's work cannot be codified into a rigid form: the term exercise can be misleading and is used here to conform with the series style. It would be inappropriate even to claim that the scores below are representative although they are intended to give a flavour of her work. In the spirit of her practice we would encourage you to make these suggestions your own, adapting and developing them in response to your circumstances, environment and experiences. Recycle the scores, develop your own resources and follow creatively wherever the explorations lead you.

Halprin's book *Dance as a Healing Art* (2000) includes extensive lesson plans and scores for using dance with people facing life-threatening illness; many of these can be applied in other situations. We recommend it for anyone wanting to explore her approach practically.

NOTE TO TEACHERS

If you want to use the following explorations in your work with others it is crucial that you take the time to experience them for yourself first, so that you teach from an experiential understanding of the approach rather than a conceptual one. Without this you will not be able to impart to your students the quality of the work which is as important as the structures presented. Please acknowledge the source of these scores when working with them.

PRACTICAL NOTES

A large uncluttered working space with natural light and air and a wooden floor is ideal. If it has immediate access to outside space especially a natural environment even better.

Wear clothes that allow freedom of movement and work with bare feet in the studio.

Have the following resources available:

- large drawing pad (A3 minimum), or newsprint or rolls of wall-paper lining paper and parcel tape (for joining sheets together), oil pastels or other drawing/painting materials (wax crayons are not very satisfactory);
- a notebook/journal and pen;
- tape recorder or CD player and appropriate music (not necessary for work in the environment).

KINAESTHETIC AWARENESS

Halprin frequently refers to the need to start work by 'inhabiting the body'. This process includes turning the attention to the physical sensations of everyday movements; heightening awareness of the rhythms of the breath and the heartbeat as experienced in the pulse and noticing information gained through all the senses. The following scores have been chosen to offer starting points for such a process with particular focus on increasing awareness of the kinaesthetic sense as described in Chapter 2. While the aim has been to select scores that are readily accessible, please adapt them according to your physical range as necessary.

MOVEMENT RITUAL 1

Movement Ritual 1, as described in Chapter 2, is a series of flowing movements that gradually bring you from lying to standing through sequences designed to activate all the functions of the spine. The movements are divided into three sections; the first based on forward and backward stretches of the spine, the second on spiral and the third on lateral movements. As well as encouraging creative and personalized use of the sequences, Halprin suggests that you always work to your 'edge'. This means taking a movement as far as is possible within your own range without experiencing pain or discomfort but with the feeling of stretching or extending fully. Increased flexibility can result from this approach over time and should not be forced through bouncing, stretching or pulling.

Exercise 4.1

Preparation

For a more detailed description of ways to prepare, you can refer to Halprin's book *Moving Towards Life: Five Decades of Transformational Dance* (1995: 41–5).

Below are examples of the type of guidelines Halprin suggests for doing Movement Ritual:

➤ Find a regular time each day to perform the movements.
➤ Choose a pleasant, aesthetically pleasing place that is private and comfortable.
➤ Stay warm but make sure there is fresh air; you could move outside.
➤ Become aware of the sounds around you and the sounds you make as you breathe and move.
➤ Alternate periods of effort with rest.

Before beginning the sequence given below, take plenty of time lying on your back to focus on the rhythm of your breathing and to become aware of which parts of the body are lying in contact with the floor. Take time to notice the four intervals of the breath: inward breath, a pause, outward breath and a pause. If these seem unclear temporarily extend the two pauses, noting when you have to take or release the breath. A process called 'palming', in which you rub your hands together to make them warm and then place the palms over the eyes with the fingers extended up into the hairline, can help to increase an inward focus on the sensations of the body. Release the hands or massage gently down the front surface of the body and then let the arms lie by your sides (Halprin 1995: 42). As you follow the movement sequences below, aim to keep your breathing full and in a steady rhythm as this helps with fluidity and the ability to extend as fully as possible into each movement. The converse, holding the breath or shallow breathing, sometimes occurs when attention is focused on the detail of the movement or on trying to achieve a set goal and this can create tension and lethargy. In order to reduce tension it is helpful to take a non-judgemental approach as you observe the capacities of your body and how these change day by day.

The following score is excerpted from Halprin's 1979 edition of the book *Movement Ritual* and should be read in conjunction with the drawings of the whole sequence created by Charlene Koonce. It follows the section on forward and backward flexion of the spine and is the first in the spiral series of movements (fifth line down in the series illustration, see Figure 4.2). It is reproduced here as an accessible sequence that encourages opening up of the ribcage, increasing lung capacity. Halprin continues to explore and change the movements, so the instructions below represent one point on her journey with Movement Ritual.

MOVEMENT 5: SPIRAL ROTATION OF THE SPINE

1. How does your body feel now? Scan your body with the breath and get in touch with any parts that are holding on. Breathe out and let go. Relax. Appreciate and enjoy any renewed energy you feel.

2. Lift your thighs to full hip flexion. Let the lower legs and feet relax. Let your legs hang out to the sides. Open up the distance between your thighs.

3. Keep your legs high in full hip flexion, then pull one leg to the side, leading with the knee. Drag your other leg, keeping open in the thighs.

4. Drop your upper leg to meet the lower leg.

5. Your head is facing away from your legs. Your shoulders are on the ground.

6. Reach and let your upper leg swing out. Draw the top knee over the bottom knee to attain greater length in your lower back. Rotate your upper leg out to attain even greater length. Stretch.

7. Bring your leg back in. Rest.

8. Reverse to the other side. Lift your upper leg. Keep open at the thighs. Pull.

9. Open and repeat this movement many times. Keep your shoulders on the ground. Breathe into the movement.

(Halprin 1979: 28–9)

Figure 4.1 Movement Ritual 1, illustrations by Charlene Koonce, 1979 (first print 1975). Images are from Halprin's *Movement Ritual* book pp. 28–9 reduced

Take time to rest before going into any of the developments suggested below.

Further explorations

Based on the sequence you have just done from Movement Ritual 1, you can begin to explore means of varying the movements through focusing on essential elements of dance – space, time and force. Choose music to accompany the following variations.

Space

Repeat the movements on the floor but this time with specific attention to the space you are travelling through. Become aware of the shapes you are making in space, and the space between you and other parts of your environment (e.g. between your right foot and the wall or your head and

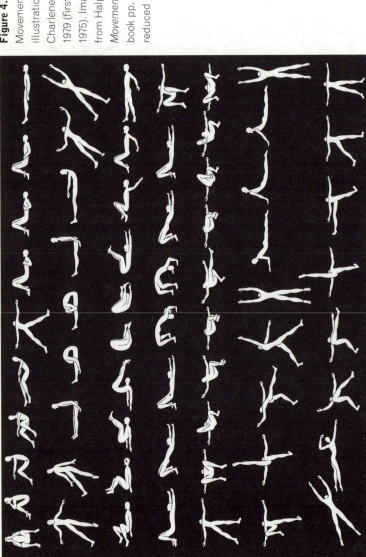

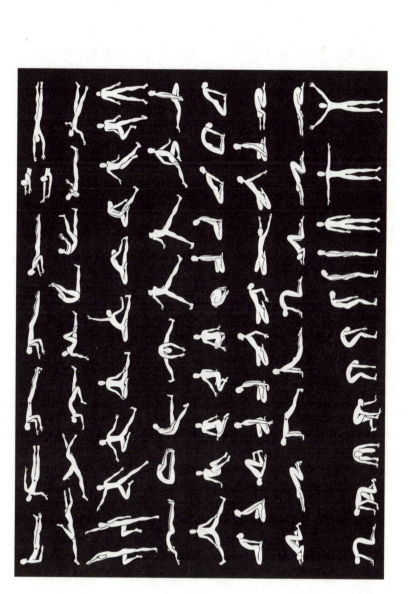

a chair). You could imagine that one part of your body leaves a coloured trail as you move and visualize the pattern it makes in the air and along the ground. Change level and explore the spiral movements in the spine on all fours and upright.

Time
Keep exploring on different levels but this time with the focus on changing the timing of the movements. Create your own short sequence of movements based on the resources above, repeat this several times in different rhythms. Observe any changes in your physical sensations, feelings or imaginative response as you experiment with changing the rhythm of your movement.

Force
What is the minimum energy necessary to accomplish one movement in the sequence? Experiment with increasing the energy you use, to discover the range of force you can apply to achieve the same movement. If you resist the movement by bringing opposing muscles into action rather than releasing them, how does this alter the dynamic quality of the action?

There are any number of variations you can try by working with differing combinations of the above.

TOWELLING

Towelling is an exercise used by Halprin in a variety of contexts (healing, training and workshops) to induce a sense of complete relaxation. Like Movement Ritual it encourages a strong sense of inner awareness, but in this instance the participant observes the movements of their own body without controlling them. One partner gently manipulates their partner's limbs using a towel to support the part of the body worked upon (hence the term 'towelling'). Although this technique shares some similarities to massage, the use of the towel creates an indirect means of contact between partners, which helps to allay anxieties that can arise when using hands directly to move someone else's body. In addition, the support is given along a greater surface area of a limb than could be achieved using hands alone and this can increase the receiver's feelings of security. The combination of increased support and decreased potentially intrusive hand contact, leaves the receiver free to focus on the sensations of movements created for them by their partner.

You will need a warm space in which half the group can lie down comfortably with room for their partners to move around them. Try to work with a partner of about the same size as yourself. Each pair will need a medium-sized towel.

The following is an adaptation of the section for working with the arms taken from Halprin's instructions for towelling in her book *Dance as a Healing Art* (2000). Towelling for the arms has been selected here since they are the lightest limbs to move. The experience of working with them can build the confidence necessary to go on to work with other parts of the body (see Halprin 2000: 138–9 for the full score for head, arms and legs). While following the instructions below it is important to remain sensitive to any indications the passive partner might give of their experience. For instance if you sense resistance to a particular movement always move away from that point, so that your partner remains relaxed and comfortable. Similarly, if the active partner finds the easiest way to lift the arm without strain, this will increase the confidence of the receiving partner.

Exercise 4.2

One person lies on the floor and relaxes (A) while the other (B) spreads the towel flat on the floor next to A's arm. B places A's arm on the middle of the towel and begins by pulling the towel gently along the floor in different directions. Then, in order to lift the arm, ensure that it is on the centre of the towel before picking up both ends of the towel to support the limb off the ground.

> Arms: Place the towel at the elbow or wrist joint. Lift the arm and rock it back and forth in the shoulder socket. Move the arm up and then slowly drop it. Raise the arm above the head and watch its stretch affect the entire ribcage. Cross the arm over the chest and draw it over the body until the shoulder blade opens, and further until the upper body rolls onto its side. Passive partner release arm to the ground. Let your arm be heavy. Carefully experiment with other ways you can move A's arms. Observe in detail how you are being an outer force moving your partner and how the movement operates in your body. Switch arms. When finished, brush towel over the arms.

(Halprin 2000: 138)

When finished separate from your partner and give her/him time to absorb the experience. This could include several minutes moving in response to the towelling with restful music if desired.

The process is then reversed so that B becomes the receiver and A actively moves B using the towel. Halprin suggests that rather than just watching B after towelling is finished, A join in the dance as B integrates their experience into movement.

Finally take your art materials and use colour and shape to freely express your experience of being moved in this way or draw any images that might have arisen. Alternatively write about the experience in your journal.

GRAVITY, INERTIA AND MOMENTUM

In her teaching Halprin makes regular reference to the forces of gravity, inertia and momentum. An understanding of these in relation to movement, like an understanding of anatomy, can provide the dancer with resources to explore a greater range of movement. She urges workshop participants to experiment with ways that they can harness these external forces to enhance their pleasure and ability in movement. The activity of towelling described above could offer a starting point for this exploration since both active and passive partners have the opportunity to observe the action of gravity and momentum on themselves and on someone else's body. The swinging action begun in towelling could be expanded in standing to observe the way that momentum increases the higher the arm swings (Halprin 1979: 9).

Rising up from lying is an example of working with overcoming inertia: the simple act of repeatedly moving between lying and standing enables the participant to observe how the force of gravity works on the body and to experiment with the degree of force necessary to counteract it. Halprin suggests further exploration of this through running in one direction and then suddenly turning to go the other way (Halprin 1979: 9).

Exercise 4.3: Rising and Falling

Whether in the context of teaching heightened kinaesthetic awareness or within the far more emotionally laden setting of working with participants of *Dancing with Life on the Line* (see Chapter 3), Halprin works with a variety of scores using rising and falling.

The following score suggests ways of physically exploring the theme of rising and falling. The first part is based on Halprin's evolutionary rise and fall.

1 Stand with your feet hip width apart, your soles spread on the floor. Feel the length of your spine rising up through the crown of your head towards the sky and drawing down through your tail-bone between your feet to the centre of the earth.

2 Releasing your breath, allow the weight of your head to drop forward. Soften in your chest. Let the weight of your head slowly lead your spine forward. Release your shoulders, allow your arms to hang. Feel the curve in your spine opening up the space between your vertebrae. Tuck your tail under and allow your knees to bend.

3 Continue to release slowly downwards until you arrive in a squatting position. Your knees near or tucked into your armpits, your head hanging. Taking your weight on your hands if necessary. Keep releasing your breath.

4 Slide your hands forward along the floor, taking your weight on your forearms until you drop gently onto you knees. Lengthen your toes so the tops of your feet are on the floor. Drop your bottom towards your heels so your body is folded, your chest touching your thighs, your head and arms resting on the floor. Breathe.

5 Lengthening your left arm and your right leg a little slowly pour your weight to the left until you are lying on your left side. Explore this until you can find a way of doing it smoothly and comfortably.

6 Roll over onto your back, lengthening your legs and opening your arms to the sides as you do so. Release your breath and allow the weight of your body to melt into the ground. Rest.

7 Reverse the journey to come up to standing. Keep your movement smooth and slow. Feel the lower and upper halves of your body unfolding together. Your tail pulls down to the ground as you uncurl your spine, feel each vertebra stack on top of the one below. Your head comes up last finding a point of balance on top of the spine.

8 Feel the length of your spine. Pushing down through the soles of your feet, allow your arms to float up at your sides, upper arms, elbows, lower arms, wrists and hands. Feel your body extending from between your shoulder blades out to the sides.

9   Let your arms continue to rise towards the sky following them with your eyes. Pushing down with your feet gently reach upwards feeling your whole body lengthen. Remember to breathe.

10   Allow your arms to float back down to your sides, keeping the sense of length in your body, feeling the space between your pelvis and your ribcage.

11   Use this as a starting point for a free exploration of rising and falling. Explore different journeys between the floor and standing, using different movement qualities and degrees of muscle tone in your body. The exploration above encourages a sense of melting into the ground. Other options might include pushing away from the floor with a degree of force or attempting to rise against strong resistance. Include your voice.

12   Vary the speed and dynamic/rhythm of your movement. For example, fall suddenly or with a staccato rhythm or repeat the cycle of rising and falling at speed.

13   Allow different parts of your body to lead you up or down. Explore one part of your body leading you in one direction while another body part resists the movement.

14   Interrupt your journeys, coming part of the way up or down and then returning.

15   Be aware of any feelings, images and associations that arise during your explorations. Take time in stillness at the end of your exploration to become aware of the sensations in your body and return to your breathing. Use the art materials or your journal to express your experiences. Then share these with a partner taking care to receive your partner's experiences without judgement.

BODY PART EXPLORATION

The following exploration of the feet is intended to give the reader an introductory experience of working with a number of different elements in the Life / Art Process including the three levels of awareness and psychokinetic visualizations. The feet have been selected as a starting point for an exploration which could be developed through all the body parts culminating in a full self-portrait visualization and performance. Equally similar explorations can be devised for any other part of the body, for example the hands, arms (towelling as described above could be included here), ribcage, legs, pelvis, spine (perhaps incorporating the sequence from Movement Ritual described on pp. 150–1) or the head.

Exercise 4.4

Anatomical Exploration

Here are some suggestions to help you become more familiar with the anatomical structure of your feet.

➤ Spend some time exploring the structure of your feet with your hands, first with your eyes shut then with them open. Feel all the different textures and forms. Try to imagine the shape of the bones. Move your feet to help you locate the joints and feel the muscles working. Feel all the different parts of your foot and the interrelationship between them: the ball of your foot, your heel, the arch of your foot, each of your toes, the top of your foot, how your foot connects to your leg through the ankle joint. What differences do you notice between your two feet?

➤ Draw your feet as accurately as you can as a result of this exploration. When you have finished compare your drawing with a detailed picture of the structure of the foot in an anatomy book. If you can obtain an anatomy colouring book (there are several available), colour in all the pictures that relate to the feet.

➤ With a partner give each other a simple foot massage with the intention of getting to know your feet better. This can be done simultaneously.

Movement Explorations

➤ Walk barefoot on different surfaces, for example grass, sand, in water, on beach pebbles. Notice all the sensations you experience in your feet.

➤ Stand and notice how you naturally place your feet on the floor. How far apart are they? Do they turn in or out? Are they symmetrical? Is your weight equally distributed on each foot or is there more weight on one of them. Don't judge or 'correct' them, just notice.

➤ Shake your feet out, stretch and flex them, circle them and rotate them in and out. Rise on to the ball of one foot and then press down with the heel and rise onto the ball of the other foot. Alternate.

➤ Put on some music with a lively and clearly defined rhythm, for example African dance music or drumming, and dance to it barefoot really feeling the soles of your feet on the floor.

➤ Explore walking in the studio in different ways and notice how you experience your feet differently if, for example:

   – you walk slowly allowing the soles of your feet to sink into the ground and connecting your breath to the soles of your feet;
   – you lead with different parts of your foot for example your heels or your toes;
   – you walk fast with your feet skimming the surface of the floor;
   – you walk with the soles of your feet slapping noisily on the floor.

   Find your own variations.

➤ Explore different qualities and speeds of moving focusing on your feet. For example: running, moving quickly and lightly covering a lot of ground hardly letting your feet touch the floor, dragging your feet, leaping, jumping making a loud exhalation as you hit the floor and letting the momentum of the movement bounce you back up, stamping, moving on your tiptoes, kicking, different rhythms of movement with different parts of your foot leading or touching the floor or making different patterns on the floor. Give one another different variations to explore. Which of these movements are familiar or unfamiliar? How do your feelings change when you move in these different ways. Do they evoke different images or associations?

➤ Let your feet explore freely and follow whatever types of movement come from them, letting the rest of your body become fully involved while the focus remains on your feet. Notice not only the sensations you feel in your feet but also any associations, images or feelings that arise. When you have finished take a few moments to absorb these.

Visualizations and Writing

➤ Draw your experience of moving from your feet. Do not try now to be anatomically correct but use shape and colour to represent how you experienced your feet. Draw both feet, they may not be the same. When you have finished, add to your drawing single words or phrases which represent the sensations, images and feelings which you experienced, or which describe what you see in your visualization.

➤ In your journal write a dialogue with your feet letting them 'speak' freely in the first person without censoring what they have to say to you. If you experience a difference on the two sides, the left and right foot might want to speak independently. If you get stuck, you might want to ask them a question.

➤ Share your drawing and your dialogue with a partner. What connections do you make between your experiences and your life? Do not judge your partner's experiences or attempt to interpret them, just be an attentive listener.

Feet Dance

➤ Spend some time reflecting on what you have discovered from your feet explorations. What attracts your attention: elements of your drawings, a colour, shape or image, phrases from your dialogue, particular ways of moving? Choose a movement quality and/or activity, an image and a phrase that you feel are connected (even if you are not sure how) and which you would like to focus on further.

➤ Put your drawing up or out on the floor and, while your partner witnesses, create a foot dance using these resources as your starting points, combining them in any way you feel moved to. Vocalize your phrase as part of your dance. Let your dance evolve freely, incorporate any associations and new material that arises. If you get stuck, look at your drawing for inspiration.

➤ When you have finished take a moment to digest your experience creating a new drawing or writing in your journal. Then share your experience with your partner. If you were the witness, tell your partner without judgement or interpretation what you saw (factual movement observations), and any images or feelings that arose for you as you witnessed their dance.

➤ Reflect on how these experiences relate to your daily life. Do you normally feel connected to your feet? Do they make a particular behaviour pattern clearer for you? For example, are you always in a hurry, or do you tend to walk on your toes to avoid being intrusive? Is there some simple action you would like to take as a result of your explorations, for example paying more attention to your feet by having a foot massage or foot spa once a week, or practising putting your feet more clearly and firmly on the ground as you walk?

➤   How would you like to develop the material you have discovered artistically? A short performance inspired by your feet? A particular character or image which has emerged and which you could develop further physically? A story that wants to be told? Take the time to follow what interests you, working either alone or with other members of your group.

MOVEMENT IN THE NATURAL ENVIRONMENT

The following suggestions serve as an introduction to Halprin's approach to working in the natural environment as described in Chapter 2. We suggest you follow the scores in the order they are presented. The work on Power Spots serves as a preparation for the Contact, Explore, Respond sequence, while the Sensory Awareness Journey moves into group work but each can stand alone. Halprin's work, based on respect for the environment, the awareness of your body and your surroundings engendered by these initial explorations, helps to ensure that you work respectfully with nature. It is important that the environment is not damaged by the work. For this work you will need clothes and shoes that you can get wet and dirty.

POWER SPOTS

Halprin refers to special places in nature to which she has returned repeatedly both as a child and as an adult as places of replenishment and creative inspiration. This may be a specific spot such as a particular tree or place on a mountain or a larger area like Sea Ranch. When the Tamalpa training programme was based at Halprin's home on the sides of Mount Tamalpais, she would encourage students to find a spot in the redwood trees surrounding the dance deck that would become a personal power spot. A place where they could spend time alone in nature, a place for quiet reflection, time out, creative replenishment or integration. Like the creative journals students were encouraged to keep during the training (which included a daily log, a section for personal reflections/writing and a dream journal), these power spots helped ground students during the intense personal and creative experiences of the training programme.

Exercise 4.5

To find your own power spot choose a place in nature close to your home, or place of work or study, which provides you with a sense of well-being where you can be undisturbed. If you are working elsewhere on a specific creative project you may want to choose a spot for the duration of that project. You may immediately know somewhere you would like to adopt as your power spot, somewhere in the environment you feel drawn to or where you would like to spend time, indeed you may already have such a place. Or you may want to wander in an area you know, opening your awareness and senses until you find somewhere that intuitively feels 'right'. You may have a sense of the place choosing you rather than the other way round. Once you have found your spot, you simply need to allow yourself to spend time there, you do not need to do anything. The following suggestions may help you 'arrive' in your power spot.

➤ Allow yourself to find a position that your body feels comfortable in, of course this may change on different occasions. Don't restrict yourself to conventional positions: if you want to lie on the earth or climb up into a tree do so. Find a position in which your body is supported so that you can release more fully.
➤ Give yourself time to quieten down and to slow down, to recognize where you are, both in your inner landscape and in the environment.
➤ Be aware of your breathing.
➤ Open all your senses, notice what you see, the colours, shapes and movements, the sounds you are aware of, the feel of the wind, sun or rain on your skin, the textures around you, the contact of your body with the environment, its weight and the imprint it makes.
➤ Once you have 'landed' in your power spot, allow whatever needs to happen. You may just to need to be still and quiet, even sleep, or you may want to move or write or draw or sing.

Anything is possible but remember you do not have to achieve or produce anything or create an agenda, this is personal time out to be in touch with yourself in nature. This may allow you to contact or release feelings of which you were unaware, creative ideas or images may arise, or answers to questions or decisions you need to make in your life may become apparent. Whatever happens this time is valuable in itself and will allow you to deepen both your connection to nature and to yourself.

Figure 4.3 *Still Dance*, 'Anna Halprin Straw Series', 1999. Photograph © Eeo Stubblefield

Your relationship with your power spot will be strengthened if you spend time there regularly becoming familiar with it at different times of day and in different seasons and weather conditions.

CONTACT, EXPLORE, RESPOND

Exercise 4.6

This exploration can be done alone or individually in the context of a group.

Choose an element in the natural environment that you would like to explore in more depth. This will obviously depend on the environment in which you are working but could include for example: rock, earth, tree, water, beach pebbles or wind. Of course all the elements in the environment are interconnected and in some situations you may find yourself working with more than one element. Similarly, although it is important that time is given for each phase of this sequence, the boundaries between them are fluid and they inevitably merge into one another.

Contact

In this phase immerse yourself in your chosen element, making physical contact with it and opening all your senses. Essentially this is a receptive and preparatory phase, it is not goal orientated. It is important that you give yourself enough time for your perception to expand beyond your daily life awareness and to allow a more organic sense of time to evolve rather than one that is dictated by a busy schedule.

Spend time in stillness in physical contact with the element you have chosen, have a sense of releasing your body and opening your senses. According to the element you have chosen you may, for example:

➤ release your weight into the earth, letting your body sink into it, noticing the imprint it makes as you surrender your weight, smelling the grass, aware of the movements it makes in the breeze. Or
➤ wrap your body round a tree feeling the surface of the bark against your cheek, noticing the tiny creatures crawling in it, listening to the creaking of the branches. Or
➤ mould your body around a rock allowing it to support your weight, feeling the roughness of its texture, its nooks and crannies, the way the light catches the wet surface.

Pay attention with all your senses to the element you are working with. Remember to use your whole body to make contact not just your hands. Change your body position experiencing different parts of your body in contact with the element and exploring the relationship between the contours of your body and its forms. As you change your position your perception will change, you will be aware of different sensations and parts of your body and will notice different details in the environment. There is no need to analyse your experience or to attempt to describe it, just be present and notice what you are aware of. You may like to make a drawing of the element you are working with as another way of heightening your perception of it.

Explore

This is a more active phase of exploration that develops out of the previous one. Once your connection to your chosen element has been established you begin to interact with it through movement.

Explore the movement activities and qualities that the environment suggests or invites. Don't try and work these out beforehand but let your body lead you in an experiential exploration interacting physically with the environment.

Explore all the physical possibilities the element offers you. Allow yourself to roll, crawl, climb, wriggle, stretch, reach, run or push, to bury, dig, lift, carry or sculpt. Engage your whole body in these activities. Give yourself permission to play physically, follow your impulses and trust your intuition, resist the temptation to undermine your experience by criticizing what you are doing. You may include your voice as part of your movement.

Respond

In this phase you allow the images, feelings and personal associations evoked by your work with the element to surface, working with them more consciously by integrating them into your physical work and beginning to work creatively with the personal mythology that emerges.

More than an open exploration, you may now focus on the movements or activities that have personal resonances for you or images that were strong. Initially, rather than analysing their meaning, commit yourself to working physically with these resources as fully as possible allowing them to develop in more depth.

For example, if the image of a bird arose as you were perched on top of a rock, allow your body to explore the movements of this bird, its movement qualities, activities, rhythms and calls, until you can embody it fully. Imagine its shape and colour, its story.

Or if you find yourself rolling heavy rocks across the beach and arranging them in a particular configuration, don't question it but allow yourself to become completely absorbed in this activity noticing your feelings or associations until you feel the task is complete. Then see what you need to do next. Rest? Place yourself within the configuration in a particular way? Dance within it? Trust your impulses.

There is no need to analyse what you are doing, simply allow the meaning to emerge from the work in its own time. After moving, you can use drawing or writing creatively in your journal to clarify the personal mythology evoked. For example you may write the bird's story using its own voice or create a drawing of it. You may then want to enter another cycle of work developing it further.

If you are working alongside other people, sharing your experiences or supporting each other's work by witnessing can enhance your understanding of the personal story or meaning embodied in it. If you are working alone, writing or drawing at the end of the session can be a helpful way to begin to integrate the material that has arisen into your daily life.

Remember to allow yourself enough time for each phase of the cycle.

You may choose to follow the cycle again with a contrasting element in the environment perhaps on another occasion. This will offer you different sensory experiences and elicit different movement qualities, evoking different images, personal associations and feelings. Try to avoid preconceptions about what the new element will offer but let it emerge from your experiences.

GROUP WORK IN NATURE

The following is a simple score suitable for any group size with the optimum being between 12 and 20. The aim is to encourage the heightening of a multi-sensory awareness of the natural environment developing into a creative response to it. The impact of the score is dependent on peeling away habitual movements and attitudes through encouraging greater receptivity to the multitude of stimuli present in the landscape. Consistent with much of Halprin's work it is the immediacy of experience that is stressed in the following score; with a refocusing of attention away from everyday personal preoccupations towards saturation in sensations generated by the environment.

You will need plenty of time for this score, a minimum of one and a half hours. The theme is 'journey'.

Exercise 4.7: Sensory Awareness Journey

➤ Choose a route through a park or open land preferably over a variety of terrain/vegetation and with as few other walkers as possible. Each participant must be aware of the route and when doing the score should be within sight of at least two other members of the group.

➤ Walk along the route without speaking to each other and become aware of the sounds, temperature, wind, changing surface structure of the ground, smells, colours, light and changing perspectives as you travel.

➤ At any time along the route, break out of walking to move in response to the stimuli around you e.g. run, scramble, swing, jump, roll, creep, hide etc. Include vocal sound.

➤ After about half way begin to notice points in the environment that seem to form gateways or entrances. Allow these observations to feed your physical exploration, so for instance enter through a gap between two trees or an arch formed by bushes. Keep playing with the images of entries, exits and doorways. If the land is open or rocky you might like to explore points of entry and exit along lines or boundaries marked by changes in terrain.

➤ Continue on your own or begin to communicate with others in the group using sounds and movement rather than words. Allow these moments of interaction to arise and fall away without any necessity to extend them into narrative.

➤ Wait quietly at the end of the route for all to return.

➤ Take time to write or draw in response to the experiences you have had and to share these with the whole group. Notice how your own response interweaves with others, the similarities and differences. This awareness is helpful in alerting you to the dual operation of creative cycles, the individual and the group.

Variations

➤ The first two instructions can be done within a shorter time scale as a way of journeying to a particular site where you wish to work. This acts as preparation for working outside.

➤ The first two instructions can be done as a running score with the focus on the changing terrain underfoot. Try running through places that you would normally avoid e.g. mud, puddles, long grass and bracken, or across a stream. Try changing the speed of the run, the length of the stride, lowering your centre of gravity as you run or the quality of impact of feet on the ground.

➤ Instead of the fourth instruction, try building structures in the environment out of the fallen materials you find there. Take care that you do not cause damage to your surroundings in doing this. You can work as a group, several groups or individually on this. Remember to dismantle and replace all materials when you finish.

GROUP WORK

Throughout her career Halprin has emphasized the constructive aspects of working in a group. She values the enriching process of collective creativity for both the group output and individual experience. It can benefit the individual through increasing energy, helping to sustain individual focus and effort, stimulating a variety of movement resources and providing a safe community for support and reflection. In order to promote these and other positive elements of group work many skills are necessary. The following scores have been chosen as ones that are fundamental to Halprin's work, occurring in slightly modified forms in a variety of contexts ranging from large-scale community performances, student training to work with people living with life-threatening illnesses. Each score offers an open-ended creative exploration that can be developed readily into further work. In addition the content and suggestions for valuaction in the scores require each participant to reflect on their personal response to the performance of instructions within the context of the group. The aim is to enable participants to increase the range of skills that allow them to contribute fully to the group process while staying alert to their own creative impetus.

THE PULSE

Halprin works with the pulse, a term that encompasses several meanings, as the basis for many scores. Some scores begin with finding your own pulse by placing your fingers lightly on the side of the neck or the wrist to feel the throb in the arteries of the heart pumping blood around the body. In other scores 'pulse' refers to the regulating beat in music or as a verb meaning to move or bounce with a steady beat. The following score is useful for starting group work or to revitalize the body after, for instance, doing Movement Ritual 1 or breathing exercises that require greater internal attention.

The score below is taken from a version of 'the Pulse' included in Halprin's book *Dance as a Healing Art* forming the second part of a workshop after a breathing meditation.

Exercise 4.8

THE PULSE

[. . .]

Have fun, energetic music playing as the group returns. This will create a high-energy atmosphere. Without speaking, initiate holding hands and make a circle.

1.   Let the leader spontaneously begin to do a pulsing movement and non-verbally ask the group to join.
2.   Stand firmly on your feet, relax your body, and initiate a pulsing movement by bouncing from your knees and allowing the impact of this bounce to travel through your whole body.
3.   Check that your knees are directly over the feet rather than turning in or out.
4.   Spread your toes apart and balance the weight of your body evenly throughout the soles of your feet. Contact the ground firmly.
5.   Check the posture of your spine. Most people have a natural 's' shape with a slight curve in the lumbar region and the neck. Find and keep this posture, and feel the bounce move softly through your spine directly from the ground to the top of your head.
6.   Keep releasing the tension in your body so that the force of the pulse will spontaneously jiggle your shoulders, the back of your neck, and travel freely through the vertebrae in your spine.
7.   Experiment with doing the pulse at different speeds. Double the time, triple it, or slow it down.
8.   Ask people to improvise and find their own variations. Pick someone out from the group and use a follow-the-leader form, until someone else in the circle finds a variation and the others pick it up and do it together.
9.   Rest.

(Halprin 2000: 55–6)

Variations

The following are suggestions for other ways of working with an emphasis on the pulse. Start with finding your own pulse in your wrist or neck and use this beat to regulate your walk. Once this is established clearly you can begin to walk in pairs or small groups. Observe how you managed to walk together. Before you finish check your pulse. How does it compare with the rhythm of the walk in a group?

Use the rhythm of your own pulse to regulate other movements such as hopping, opening and closing the hands, skipping or pushing, and track how the pulse changes speed as you perform increasingly energetic movements. What is it like to move in opposition to the beat of your pulse?

Observe how large a movement you can make within one beat (taken from music or continuing with heart rate as guide) and compare the speed of this with a very small movement made within the same time. Work with a partner or in small groups with any of these resources as the starting point for an exploration.

For an example of a more developed score that focuses initially on the pulse compare the above with the 'Vortex' outlined in Chapter 3.

TRAILS

This score for increasing trust and intimacy in a group is included in '*Circle the Earth*: A Search for Living Myths and Rituals' (1995) an unpublished manual by Halprin with Rachel Kaplan. As pointed out in the introduction to this score, the demand for direct physical contact poses a challenge for some groups or individuals who are not accustomed to working in this way. To help counteract fear or self-consciousness it is important to establish guidelines based on each participant taking care as they move along the trail and that the whole group works in a non-judgemental way. Since the person moving along the trail is blindfolded you have to rely on the kinaesthetic sense and each participant is encouraged to use many parts of their body to trace their way, rather than just hands.

As the groups become more confident, they can experiment with various ways of making the trails using different levels and shapes. Whoever travels along the trail should be given the time they need to complete the task without the expectation that they will be faster as the sequence continues.

Exercise 4.9

Intention: To build trust and intimacy

Expand range of movement possibilities

Interact with people through touch

Score

Time: 30 minutes

Space: Throughout the room in lines

People: Working in groups

1.   Blindfold one person.
2.   Form a linear path away from the blindfolded person with the rest of the group, using all levels (standing, bending, kneeling, sitting, lying) and staying in physical contact with the person in front of and behind you.
3.   When this 'trail' is in place, the blindfolded person follows it out to the end by moving from one body to another along the line.
4.   Remove the blindfold and look at the path you've travelled.
5.   Share your one strongest image and feeling with your group.
6.   Put the blindfold on another member of the group, form a new trail, and repeat the score until everyone has performed it.

(Halprin with Kaplan 1995: 36)

LEADING AND FOLLOWING

Halprin notes that one of the values of this score is in the teaching of skills that enable performers to relate effectively with one another. Through physical experience of each role, participants can assess their own preference for one mode or another and explore the potential offered by less familiar roles. 'Blending' refers to two people moving with such clear lines of communication and attentiveness that they are barely able to tell who is leading and when this switches. As skills increase this can happen at speed and with varying distances between the partners. Halprin's scores frequently apply simultaneously to several aspects of the performance process. This is shown by the following score that can generate resources and stimulate an increased movement range for each participant, as well as encouraging the performer to develop flexibility in response to moving with others.

Exercise 4.10

Intention: Learn to lead, follow and blend with another person

Score

Time: 2 hours

Space: Scattered through the room

People: In partners and switching partners

1. Sit in partners, one person close eyes. The other person keep eyes open and using only their hands, lead partner into movement. The person with eyes closed place palms on top of hands of the person who leads.
2. On the signal, switch roles.
3. Switch partners.
4. Stand up in place and lead your partner's movement, engage the legs. Use only vertical movement (up and down). On the signal, switch roles.
5. Stop and share how it feels to follow or to lead. Do you have a preference?
6. Find new partners. Both people keep eyes open, alternate active and passive roles and move through space. Use whole body. Switch roles when signalled.
7. Change partners again. Continue the exercise, this time each person use different degrees of active/passive (on a scale of 1–10, 1 being completely limp, 10 being totally active and the numbers in between representing various degrees of motion).
8. With the same partner, change from active to passive roles without an outside signal being given.

(Halprin with Kaplan 1995: 66)

Variations

There are many starting points for active/passive work in partners. You could develop these yourselves using familiar games or theatre exercises that demand an active and a passive role, for instance mirroring in pairs or moulding a partner as if they are clay. It can be helpful to ask pairs to freeze in position and change active/passive roles from the place they find themselves in, so that the whole body is used for moulding rather than just the hands. This also helps ease into the next stage of blending when pairs move without an outside signal to change role.

After exploring passive, active and blend leave time to discuss the experience. Which role did you prefer? Were you able to move easily between roles? How would you describe the experience of blending? What movement resources did you gain from working with your partner that you would like to explore further?

Finally, you could consider how the skills learnt here could help you in working with the longer 'Vortex' score outlined in Chapter 3.

GROUP RITUALS

The ritual aspect of Halprin's work has been discussed in depth in Chapter 3 it is important to note here that ritual elements can play a part in any session if required. Halprin refers to 'ritual consciousness' as the means by which you 'notice the potential ritual in your everyday experience . . .' (Halprin 2000: 40) and she suggests that use of ritual and ceremony can enrich individual and group experience. For instance a ritual opening or ending for a group that meets weekly can help to mark the time as set aside from everyday business. The following is a simple example from a workshop on ritual making given by Halprin (2002b). Each participant was registered for the course at the gate by the road. Without further instructions it was clear that once you entered the gate and descended the long flight of steps through the trees, down to the lounge, the process of the day was underway. Halprin indicated that each space, gate at road, lounge, studio and dance deck, marked a different function in the process of the day. Awareness of this delineation helped focus the group and clarify expectations (social interaction in lounge, work on ritual in studio and deck).

Rather than suggest rituals here it is more appropriate for your group to decide on whether a ritual element is relevant and work together to create your own. The process of creating a ritual can help develop a strong sense of group identity and shared values. Starting with something very simple, such as a way of marking the end of a workshop, can lead to more complex rituals that reflect significant points in the group.

Below are some suggestions for creating a ritual for a group.

Exercise 4.11

➤   What is the focus of the group? You could devise a ritual opening for the session that marks the reason that you are working together and your personal connection to this. This could be done through creating a simple group rhythm or through each person contributing to the decoration of the space or a group sculpture.

➤ Halprin often works with food rituals. If you do not want to break the connection of the group in the course of a day workshop, you could devise a ritual for creating a special space for eating and presentation of food. Decide whether you are going to prepare without speaking and set a time for preparation.

➤ There might be a transition point in the group's work that could be highlighted through the creation of a ritual. We can, as Halprin describes, 'invest the objects of our daily lives with new significance' (Halprin 2000: 42). Choose one object to represent the past work you are finishing and another to show the fresh direction the group is taking. How might you place these to show the shift in focus of the group?

➤ If you want to mark the ending of a group or one person leaving, it could be appropriate to consider how the work will be integrated into your life and create a ritual that allows each person to express this.

For an example of a large-scale community ritual see the score for the 'Earth Run' in Chapter 3.

RSVP CYCLES

The following suggestions serve as a practical introduction to one possible application of the RSVP Cycles as described in Chapters 2 and 3. This example is devised for a group of people working in an urban environment but the Cycles have the potential to be used for collaborative creative work in a wide variety of situations for many different purposes.

Exercise 4.12

As a group decide on an environment in your area in which you want to work. This should include a discussion of your motivation or intention for choosing to work in that particular place. Is it a place that is overlooked in your local environment that you would like to encourage people to appreciate more? A site of historical interest or of local contention?

A place you want to celebrate or reclaim? Are you working with a community group on an issue which is related to that environment? Or is it simply a place you want to get to know better? These are only examples, there are many other possibilities. Make sure that your discussion is inclusive, that everyone has a chance to speak and that everyone's ideas are considered. You are aiming to arrive at a consensus, something you can all agree on and commit yourselves to even if your reasons for doing so vary. You may find it helpful to visit the sites being considered and continue your discussions there.

Gathering Resources

In this exploration we are going to start the process by gathering resources although it is possible to enter the cycle at any point.

➤ Spend time familiarizing yourself with the environment, just being there, positioning yourself at different points within it. How does this change your perception and experience of the place? What do you notice? What are the atmosphere and rhythms of the place and how do they change at different times of the day? What activi-ties happen in the place? What types of people frequent it, how do they move through it and within it? Is it different at different times in the day or on different days of the week or at different times of the year? You might want to draw the environment or make a map of the site.

➤ Explore the movement possibilities offered by the physical structures of the site if you don't restrict yourself to the way they are normally used. Do this by moving through the site, over, under, and around its structures, for example sliding down, rolling along or jumping off walls, crawling under benches, hanging from or somersaulting over railings. Explore pathways through space, points of entering and leaving the site, open and contained spaces within it, different levels, boundaries within the space and the spatial relationship between different elements within it. Explore different speeds, rhythms, directions and ways of moving through the space; try running, walking backwards, leaping or moving in slow motion; try out possibilities suggested by members of the group. Be aware of your own safety and that of passers-by.

➤ Open yourselves up to the imaginative possibilities of the space, what images, themes or stories suggest themselves? This may relate to the daily life activities of the place or its history or not. There's no need to curtail your imagination at this stage.

➤ As a group, brainstorm all the resources you have gathered so far, writing them down so everyone can see them. Rolls of newsprint or lining paper are useful for this. Don't forget to include the other resources you have available, for example the amount of time you have, the number of people, any particular skills they have, any financial resources and the motivations discussed earlier.

Devising Scores

Scoring is the process by which you begin to select and shape your material.

Having agreed upon your overall intention it is likely, unless you want to create a spontaneous event, that you will create several scores in the course of your preparation. You will therefore need to decide at each stage what the purpose (intention) of each score is (an introductory score will inevitably be different from the final score for a public event). This makes it easier to select the appropriate resources and agree upon the score. For example you may decide to explore a particular theme using specific movement resources in relation to a particular area of the site in order to develop this material further. If you give yourselves the time to create a number of exploratory scores then you are not closing down your options but allowing yourselves to explore different and even contradictory possibilities in more depth. Small groups may devise scores for others in the group or for the whole group, or may perform their own scores.

Scores can include both graphics and words. There are many different ways to create scores but as an introduction two simple possibilities include:

➤ Writing a series of numbered instructions like the steps of a recipe with additional diagrams if appropriate (for example the 'Trails' and the 'Pulse' scores earlier in this chapter).

➤ Creating a visual map with simple instructions, indicating for example pathways through space and movement resources to be used (see Chapter 3, score for *The Planetary Dance*).

Guidelines for writing scores

➤ Clarify your theme and intention at the outset.
➤ Keep your scores simple and clear enough that they can be followed without further explanation.
➤ Remember scores are intended to communicate and generate creativity rather than control others.
➤ Be aware how open or closed your score is (see p. 73).
➤ Indicate *who* (how many people) the score is for, how much *time* is available to perform it and *where* it is to be performed.
➤ Be open to the fortuitous and unexpected. In a creative process you cannot score everything; in a public space this is particularly apparent. Regard the unexpected as an additional resource rather than an obstruction.

Performing Scores

Carry out the score or scores that have been devised. Remember that in this context performance is only related to theatrical performance if that is the intention of the score. Be aware if you are 'breaking' the score (not following it) and why.

Valuaction

As a group evaluate what you have done and decide what action you want to take as a result. Once again, in the same way as you did when you were gathering resources, document your valuaction clearly as you go along so that everyone can be involved.

You may consider the following in your valuaction:

➤ What worked well?
➤ What would you like to develop further?
➤ What new resources (e.g. themes, movement activities or qualities) have arisen from the score even if these are a result of something that hasn't worked as intended? Do you want to explore these further?
➤ Is the score clear? Does it need to be more open or more closed?
➤ Where do you go from here? The answer to this will depend on your overall intention and at what stage of the process you are. Do you

need to recycle this score refining it further or including additional resources? Do you want to return to your original list and create a new score based on different resources?

Notes on valuaction

➤ Valuact according to your original intention. If a score has been intended as an initial exploration do not evaluate it as a polished performance.
➤ Listen to and include everyone's responses and endeavour to reach a consensus.
➤ Be constructive.
➤ Differentiate between valuacting the score itself or the performance of the score. Resist the temptation to blame the performers if a score hasn't communicated clearly.
➤ You can valuact at any stage of the process, for example valuacting your resources before going any further, maybe there is something additional you need, or valuacting and revising your score prior to performing it.
➤ Valuaction always leads you back into the cycle, it is not the end of a linear process.

When you have completed your valuaction continue working with the cycle towards your agreed intention by devising, performing and valuacting scores using your chosen resources.

BIBLIOGRAPHY

Allsopp, R., Friedman, K. and Smith, O. (eds) (2002) 'On Fluxus', *Performance Research* 7(3).

Amirrezvani, A. (2000) 'Purposely Out of Step', *San Jose Mercury News*, 2 June.

Anderson, J. (1966) 'Dancers and Architects Build Kinetic Environments', *Dance Magazine* November: 52–6, 74.

—— (1969) 'Ferment and Controversy', *Dance Magazine* August: 47–55.

—— (1997) 'Celebrating Life after a Dance with Death', *New York Times*, 22 June.

Banes, S. (1987) *Terpsichore in Sneakers: Post-modern Dance*, Middletown, Conn.: Wesleyan University Press.

—— (1993) *Democracy's Body: Judson Dance Theater, 1962–1964*, Durham, NC: Duke University Press.

Burns, J. T. (1967) 'Experiments in Environment', *Progressive Architecture* July: 131–7.

Butler, D. and McHugh, J. (2001) 'Anna Halprin at 80', *Contact Quarterly* winter/spring.

Certificate (1997) Samuel H. Scripps, American Dance Festival Award.

Charest, R. (1987) *Robert Lepage: Connecting Flights*, trans. W. Romer Taylor, London: Methuen.

Circle the Earth (1987) Video, Melbourne Town Hall, Melbourne, 18 January.

Circle the Earth: Dancing with Life on the Line (1989) Video, Anna Halprin with Media Arts West.

Dancers' Group Studio Theater (2000) *Anna Halprin 80th Year Retrospective*, performance programme, Colwell Theater, Fort Mason, San Francisco.

80th Year Retrospective (2000) Video, Dir. Andy Abrahams Wilson.

Eiko and Koma (2002) Official website: http://www.eikoandkoma. org/ekhome.html. Site designed by E. N. Waterhouse (accessed 14 July 2003).

Embracing Earth, Dances with Nature (1995) Video, Dir. Anna Halprin, filmed by Ellison Hall and Abrahams Wilson Productions.

Feldenkrais, M. (1980) *Awareness through Movement*, Harmondsworth: Penguin.

Feliciano, R. (2000) 'Anna Halprin Celebrates Long Life and Dance Career', *San Francisco Chronicle*, 28 May.

Forti, S. (1999) 'Style is a Corset', interview by Christophe Wavelet, *Writings on Dance* 18/19, winter: 147–53.

Greskovic, R. (1999) 'Eiko and Koma' in Martha Bremser (ed.) *Fifty Contemporary Choreographers*, London and New York: Routledge: 97–9.

Gropius, W. (ed.) (1961) *The Theater of the Bauhaus*, Middletown, Conn.: Wesleyan University Press.

Halprin, A. (*c.*1938–40) Unpublished college notebooks in San Francisco Performing Arts Library and Museum archive, 11 iii Chronology, early work.

—— (1948) *Impulse*, San Francisco: Halprin–Lathorp Studio.

—— (*c.*1960s) Untitled unpublished interview notes in San Francisco Performing Arts Library and Museum archive, 11 ii Performances, theory, general notes.

—— (1969) *Collected Writings*, San Francisco: San Francisco Dancers' Workshop.

—— (1973) 'Community Art as Life Process', *The Drama Review* 17(3): 64–80.

—— (1979) *Movement Ritual*, with illustrations by Charlene Koonce, Kentfield, Calif.: Tamalpa Institute.

—— (1981) 'Discovering Dance', *Lomi Bulletin* summer: 14–18.

—— (1987) Letter to Friends of *Circle the Earth*.

—— (1988) 'Expanding Spaces', *In Dance* 15(9): 17.

—— (1992) 'What Else is There?', interview by Janice Ross, *The Drama Review* 36(1): 52–4.

—— (1995) *Moving Towards Life, Five Decades of Transformational Dance*, ed. R. Kaplan, Hanover and London: Wesleyan University Press.

—— (1997–2000) Untitled unpublished pre- and post-performance notes on *Still Dance*, Kentfield, California.

—— (2000) *Dance as a Healing Art*, Mendocino, Calif.: Life Rhythm.

—— (2001a) 'A Future Where Dance is Honoured', Roundtable keynote address *Dance Journal USA* 17(3/4): 16–17.

—— (2001b) Interviews with Helen Poynor, Kentfield, California, 25–7 June.

—— (2001c) 'Dancing on the Mountain – Moshe and the Halprin Life/Art Process', Keynote address, The Feldenkrais Guild® North America, Annual Conference: On-Site Recording Productions.

—— (2002a) Interviews with Libby Worth, Kentfield, California, 31 April–2 May.

—— (2002b) Workshop on ritual, Mountain Home Studio, Kentfield, California, 3 May.

—— and friends (1995) *The Planetary Dance* flyer, Kentfield, California.

—— and others (1975) *Second Collected Writings 1973–75*, San Francisco: San Francisco Dancers' Workshop.

—— and others (1989) *Collected Writings III*, San Francisco: Tamalpa Institute/San Francisco Dancers' Workshop.

—— and Planetary Dance Community (2002) *The Planetary Dance* flyer, Kentfield, California.

—— and San Francisco Dancers' Workshop (1977) *Citydance, 1977*, San Francisco: San Francisco Dancers' Workshop.

—— and Sea Ranch Collective (2003) *Seasons, Part 1/Summer*, performance programme, Mountain Home Studio/Theatre, Kentfield, California, June.

—— with Kaplan, R. (1995) '*Circle the Earth*, A Search for Living Myths and Rituals through Dance', unpublished, Kentfield, California.

—— with Stinson, A. (1987) *Circle the Earth* manual, unpublished, Kentfield, California.

Halprin, L. (1969) *The RSVP Cycles – Creative Processes in the Human Environment*, New York: George Braziller.

—— (1999) Interviewed by Andy Hestor, *Places* 12(2): 43–51.

Halprin Khalighi, D. (1989) *Coming Alive, The Creative Expression Method*, Kentfield, Calif.: Tamalpa Institute.

Hartley, L. (1989) *Wisdom of the Body Moving – An Introduction to Mind–Body Centering*, Berkeley, Calif.: North Atlantic Books.

H'Doubler, M. (1940) *Dance – A Creative Art Experience*, Madison, Wis.: University of Wisconsin Press.

Hering, D. (1967) 'Reviews: Dancers' Workshop of San Francisco in *Parades and Changes* Hunter College April 21–22, 1967', *Dance Magazine* June: 36–7, 72.

Howard, R. (2000a) 'Dancing Outside', *San Francisco Weekly*, May/June.

—— (2000b) 'Anna Halprin 80th Year Retrospective', *Dance Magazine* 1 November.

Kapit, W. and Elson, L. (2003) *The Anatomy Coloring Book*, New York, San Francisco, London: Canfield Press/Harper & Row.

Kaplan, R. (1992) 'Dancing with Life on the Line', *Vox Magazine* summer: 11–12.

Kaye, N. (2001) *Site Specific Art, Performance, Place and Documentation*, London and New York: Routledge.

Kerner, M. C. (1988) 'Anna Halprin – Integrating Emotion and Technique', *Dance Teacher Now* June: 12–16.

Kisselgoff, A. (2002) Dance review: 'Travel Companions on Life's Inevitable Journey', *New York Times*, late edition, Section E, 31 January: 1.

Kostelanetz, R. (1970) *The Theatre of Mixed Means*, London: Pitman Publishing.

Lawrence and Anna Halprin, Inner Landscapes (1991) Video, Dir. Joan Saffa, San Francisco Cultural Programming Dpt. KQED, Inc. (aired summer 1994).

Legacy Oral History Project (1992) *Circle the Earth, 1991 Dancing with Life on the Line* (narrators: Jerry de Jong, Mary, Jeff Regh, Brian Varanzoff), San Francisco: San Francisco Performing Arts Library and Museum.

McHugh J. (1989) 'Elemental Motion: "Dancing Myths and Rituals in Nature"', *Contact Quarterly* spring/summer: 9–10, 12–13.

McMann Paludan, M. (1995) 'Expanding the Circle: Anna Halprin and Contemporary Theatre Practice', unpublished Ph.D. thesis, University of Kansas.

Mazo, J. H. (2000) *Prime Movers*, second edition, Princeton, NJ: Princeton Book Company.

Novack, C. J. (1990) *Sharing the Dance: Contact Improvisation and American Culture*, Madison, Wis.: University of Wisconsin.

Parades and Changes (1965) Video, Dir. Arne Arneborn, National Swedish Television.

Pierce, R. (1975) 'The Anna Halprin Story', *The Village Voice* 20: 93–9, 13 March. Also in Halprin, A. and others (1975) *Second Collected Writings 1973–75*, San Francisco: San Francisco Dancers' Workshop.

Planetary Dance (2002) Community performance ritual facilitated by Anna Halprin, Mount Tamalpais, Marin, California, 4 May.

Planetary Dance Board (1988) Letter to *Circle the Earth/Planetary Dance* network.

Positive Motion (1991) Video, Dir. Andy Abrahams Wilson, San Francisco.

Rehg, J. (2001) 'Reflections on *Intensive Care* from a Performer's Point of View', *Contact Quarterly* winter/spring: 46–9.

Returning Home (2003) Video, Dir. Andy Abrahams Wilson, Sausilito, Calif.: Open Eye Pictures.

Rockwell, J. (2000) 'Bridging Past and Present', *New York Times*, 11 June.

Rolf, I. (1977) *Rolfing, the Integration of Human Structures*, New York: Harper & Row.

Roose-Evans, J. (1970) *Experimental Theatre from Stanislavsky to Today*, New York: Avon Books.

Ross, J. (1981) Review of *In and on the Mountain*, *Dance Magazine* July.

—— (2000) *Moving Lessons – Margaret H'Doubler and the Beginning of Dance in American Education*, Madison, Wis.: University of Wisconsin Press.

Rutkowski, A. (1984) 'Development, Definition and Demonstration of the Halprin Life/Art Process in Dance Education', unpublished Ph.D. thesis, International College, California.

Sandford, M. (1995) *Happenings and Other Acts*, London and New York: Routledge.

San Francisco Dancers' Workshop (*c.*1970/1) Workshop and perform-ance documentation, San Francisco.

Steinberg, J. (1986) 'Ritual Keeper – Anna Halprin', *High Performance*, 33(9): 9–12.

Stubblefield, E. (2001) *Still Dance* publicity, New York.

—— (2004a) Information on *Still Dance* website http://www.still dance.net (accessed 14 February 2004).

—— (2004b) Telephone interviews with Libby Worth, February.

Tamalpa Institute (1981) *In the Mountain, On the Mountain* programme, Kentfield, California.

—— (1984) *Run to the Mountain* programme, Kentfield, California.

—— (1985) *Circle the Mountain, a Dance in the Spirit of Peace with Anna Halprin* promotional leaflet, Kentfield, California.

—— (1985/6) Publicity brochure, Kentfield, California.

—— (1986a) Publicity for *Moving Toward Life*, Kentfield, California.

—— (1986b) *Circle the Earth – A Dance in the Spirit of Peace*, promotional leaflet, Kentfield, California.

—— (1989) *Circle the Earth, Dancing with Life on the Line*, promotional leaflet, Kentfield, California.

—— (1995) *Tamalpa Drum*, Kentfield, California, winter.

Todd, M. E. (1968) *The Thinking Body*, New York: Dance Horizons.

Ulrich, A. (2000) 'Halprin a Delight at Retrospective', *San Francisco Examiner*, 6 June.

Wolf, M. (2000) 'Dancing Solo', *Northern California Bohemia*, 14 December.

Yerna Buena Center for the Arts Theater (2002) Publicity for *Be With*, Anna Halprin, Eiko and Koma, Jean Jeanrenaud for 17–19 January 2002. E-mail (10 January 2002).

CONTACTS

ANNA HALPRIN

Email: anna@annahalprin.org
Website: www.annahalprin.org

TAMALPA INSTITUTE

PO Box 794, Kentfield
California 94914 USA
Tel.: 415/457-8555
Fax: 415/457-7960
Email: info@tamalpa.org
Website: www.tamalpa.org

UK COUNTRY CONTACT FOR TAMALPA INSTITUTE

Caroline Born
Tel.: 01548 560786
Email: heartwood@clara.co.uk

LIBBY WORTH

Email: libby.worth@rhul.ac.uk

HELEN POYNOR

WALK OF LIFE Movement
Workshops
3 Marmora Terrace
Clapps Lane, Beer
Devon EX12 3HE UK
Tel.: 01297 20624

INDEX

Notes: Please note that page references to illustrations and photographs are in *italic* print. References to major mentions of topics are in **bold** print. AH stands for Anna Halprin.